THE FIX

HOW TO ALIGN YOUR ORGANIZATION FOR GROWTH AND SUCCESS

THE FIX

HOW TO ALIGN YOUR ORGANIZATION FOR GROWTH AND SUCCESS

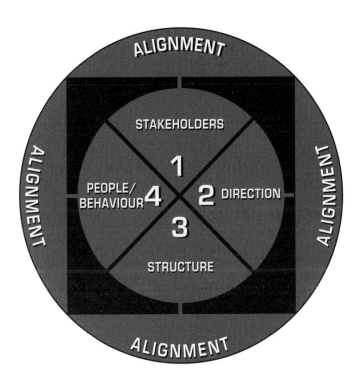

BY FRED McLEAN
AND PAUL KNOWLES

Published by **FUSION Consulting Inc.**
3 Lansdowne Park Cr.,
Box 236,
Komoka, Ontario
N0L 1R0

Cover by David B. Sapelak
Printed by Friesen Printers,
Altona, Manitoba, Canada R0G 0B0

ISBN 0-9699323-0-8

To Kate and Mary, who keep our lives in alignment, day by day.

CONTENTS

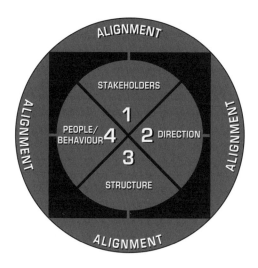

FOREWORD

Over the course of the past fifteen years I have had the privilege of working with many organizations, assisting them in their growth and dealing with many alignment questions. Our experiences have involved much trial and error, along with many invaluable opportunities to learn.

The content of this book captures these first-hand and very practical experiences and lessons. The process you will discover in this book is not a theoretical or academic concept, but rather a proven process that works. Many organizations have been working with this approach, and are reaping the rewards of 'true alignment'.

The idea of capturing this process, in a written fashion that would be of assistance to leaders in all types of organizations, has been of keen interest to me for a number of years. I have developed and implemented the concepts successfully in many situations, but I found the discipline of writing to be a significant challenge. When Paul suggested and pursued the idea of writing a book as a joint project, I found the answer to my dilemma. And from that has come this opportunity to assist those individuals with whom I may never work directly.

I would like to thank my many clients for their trust in providing me the opportunity of being of service. Over the years I have met many committed individuals who are making a difference in their chosen field of endeavour. The tasks and challenges have not been easy, but I must say that for the most part they have been very rewarding. I trust that my assistance has made a contribution in better serving the needs of my clients. In putting together this book, a number of our clients and friends assisted in providing valuable input that enhanced the final text. Thank you to those who shared opinions and insights.

I sincerely wish to thank Paul for his patience, understanding and friendship. In addition to the time and work involved in putting together this manuscript, we had many enjoyable times. It has been a satisfying and fun experience.

Finally, I wish to thank my family for their support and understanding. My wife Kate has been a partner in our business and we have experienced a beautiful working relationship, along with our strong personal ties. My daughter Linley has been a strong centre of pride and she has provided me with many rich learning experiences.

- Fred McLean

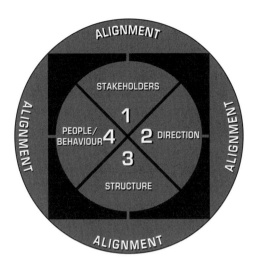

INTRODUCTION

Once upon a time, not very many years ago, Gerry Turbine had an idea. A good idea, an idea that should — in fact, he was sure, it would — make money.

So Gerry and his partner, Jim, closed their eyes, crossed their fingers, and stepped into the unknown. They mortgaged their houses, and invested that money, and their savings, in G & J Concepts Inc.

And — without the aid of a fairy godmother — it worked! G & J turned a profit within three years, Gerry and Jim hired George and Alice and Ralph and about 45 other employees, and G & J Concepts prospered.

For a while.

Today, though, Gerry and Jim are sitting at their desks, trying to figure out what went wrong. Their business has grown considerably, but they are having a number of problems. These include handling the work load from client orders; quality control of product delivered; serving their clients, particularly those with whom they have established long term, high quality relationships; morale of their staff; staff who refuse to take ownership of their jobs and responsibilities.

These issues may seem easy to identify, but they can be very difficult to solve. It can be very hard to pinpoint the source of the problem. It's a little like being stuck and sinking in quicksand — the problem is clear; the solution is not.

That is exactly where Gerry and Jim find themselves. Now, they feel like they need that fairy godmother. But apparently, fairy godmothers don't do business with small corporations.

How could such a good idea produce such a barrel-full of headaches and problems? What went wrong?

Exactly the same things that can go wrong with almost any business or organization, including yours.

G & J Concepts has shown impressive growth, but along with the growth have come an overabundance of problems. As quickly as Gerry's idea brought success, rapid change and growth have brought him major organizational challenges. In current organizational parlance, G & J has moved past the second phase, into the third phase.

(For a complete description of the three phases of growth, see page 23.)

And they have found there is no magic. Sure-fire, quick-fix solutions may seem to provide obvious answers, but it's far from certain that they have ever actually fixed anything.

But that does not mean that solutions are impossible. If Gerry, and the leaders, managers and supervisors in other struggling organizations, are willing to make some fundamental changes in their approach to business management and the way they think and act, there is real reason for hope.

This book will be a guide to help individuals and organizations find the foundational solutions. It will help any organization where there are two or more people working together. It will assist non-business organizations and even families. We have written the book in a self-help fashion and heartily encourage you to utilize the text as a step-by-step organizational development tool.

What is needed is a long-term commitment to applying foundational principles to how an organization — your organization — functions. You need to learn to adapt to changes affecting business, to adapt to changes in your organization, and to be flexible when faced with the new external forces that every organization faces, today.

The days when quick-fix solutions provided answers to corporate problems are gone. Some of the solutions worked admirably — for a while, in the short term. But for an organization to move into the 21st century, healthy, strong, and able to create its future, it must build that future on a value system that is aligned with principles that create long term effectiveness.

Your organization needs to be in alignment, to be kept tuned up. Many organizations are running like a car that is two or three years old. When it was new, it ran well. Today, it's still on the road, and it's still running, but something is wrong. The car has gotten out of alignment, and every driver knows that it is a lot tougher job to keep that vehicle heading in the right direction. This misalignment also means the tires are wearing unevenly and too quickly, the mileage is not as good as it had been, and the car is not running as smoothly as it had run in the past.

When we speak of alignment, we include the tuning up of the vehicle, as well. When you recognize signs that things are not running the way they should, such as the car pulling to one side, or the engine idling rough, or having difficulty starting the car, you need to pay attention to these signs. It's no good just to hope that things will get better.

Today, too many organizations are running just like that two-year-old car.

But, like the car, they can be fixed. In this book, we will discover a new way of building an organization, founded on time-proven principles, and then moving ahead, newly aligned, with a shared vision, heading toward a strong future.

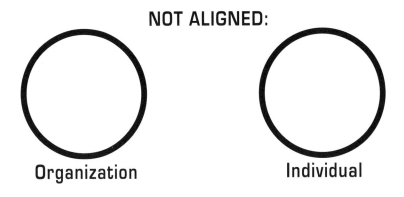

NOT ALIGNED:

Organization   Individual

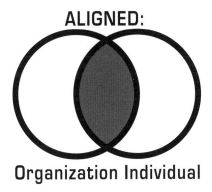

ALIGNED:

Organization Individual

This is the first key to capturing success for your organization: alignment, across the board, involving every person in your organization. When the people who are part of the corporate team share commitment and vision; when they have accepted the vision, and incorporated it into their approach to their jobs, and their business relationships, the organization is aligned.

This must be shared and understood, across the board. No matter how well you — as president, supervisor, middle manager, or employee — grasp the principles of this book, if the other members of your team don't share this new vision, you will not capture the healthy future you seek.

You will notice, in the diagram on the preceding page, that alignment does not mean that the employees of your organization have to be workaholics, totally focused on the job, with no life outside the office or plant. Too many organizations have tried to achieve success that way, only to face complete corporate burn-out. The diagram shows that the person and the organization have to be in harmony, in the area where their concerns overlap. The top diagram shows an employee who functions completely out of alignment with the organization. The bottom diagram shows the ideal situation — where the employee is an individual, with a meaningful life apart from the organization. However, when the employee is on the job, he or she is heading in the same direction as the organization. The employee shares the corporate vision. This is illustrated in the "aligned" model on the previous page, by the shaded area showing overlap between the organization and the individual.

The key to solving your corporate problems is the development, acceptance, and incorporation of that shared commitment and vision. Think back to the days when your organization began. Like G & J Concepts, it was founded on an idea, a vision. Gerry found success, initially, because he focused on that idea, developed it, and made it work.

"Shared commitment and vision" reflect an organization that is operating as a "team". A team is a group of individuals who have a common goal or goals, are applying their energies and talents in a unified fashion, and have developed a level of trust and respect for one another that surpasses any differences they may have in implementing actions. In considering the second point above, concerning application of energies or talents, the need for diversity in talents is an important ingredient for most organizations to succeed. Consider a sports team which must have the variety of skills and talents for the different positions. The element of "team work" will represent a critical ingredient for incorporating the principles and ideas within this book.

But as the organization grew, ownership of the vision did not. Responsibility became much more widely spread among the employees — as they made decisions for their own departments, as they dealt one-on-one with clients, and as they took on purchasing and product development responsibilities — but the vision remained locked inside the president's head. The employees may have been doing the best they could, but the organization had gotten out of alignment, just like a right front tire that is turning as well as it ever did, but is pulling somewhat to the right. It's working, but it is not working well, and it can lead to much more serious consequences.

His employees did not share Gerry's vision — and just as importantly, Gerry did not understand or share theirs. Not surprisingly, G & J is faltering. By "vision" we mean a shared understanding on issues such as where we, as an organization, are going; why this is important; what our objectives are. These are some of the questions that can assist individuals within an organization to work in a focused and aligned fashion.

Maybe you have had this kind of experience: you and your spouse or companion agree to go to dinner with another couple. They will pick you up at 6:30 p.m., and they'll choose the restaurant.

You have known this other couple for a while, and you

know that they are casual dressers, people who are likely to take you to a comfortable, friendly restaurant. That is your understanding — your vision — of the evening to come.

At 6:30 p.m., you answer the door in slacks and a sport shirt, and find they have arrived, he in a suit and she in a lovely evening dress. You are out of alignment, because the couples had different visions of the evening, and did not share the vision with one another.

In this case, of course, the sharing, or communication, was automatic at the moment the door opened, even if it was too late to solve the problem. But in many organizations, that moment of revelation never comes, and team members proceed for years out of alignment, each doing the best job he or she can, but not really heading in the same direction, not sharing the same vision, and — perhaps even more serious — confident that their diverse visions are really the organizational vision.

Are your employees or fellow team members on the inside, sharing your vision, or on the outside, excluded, awkward and confused?

There will never be a better time to begin sharing the important things about your organization. Because as you begin to adopt and apply the principles of this book, and share them all the way through your corporation, you will be well on the way to finding a successful path for your organization's future.

We are writing this book to present a model that will help organizations align with their major stakeholders — the individuals and organizations who have a stake in the operation and success of your organization. More about stakeholders in later chapters.

We are practicing alignment ourselves. As Fred, a corporate consultant, works with Paul, a writer, we continually check our alignment, we regularly communicate to be sure that we share the same vision, that we are attempting to accomplish the same goals. We meet, telephone and communicate by modem constantly, to be sure we are heading in exactly the same direction on each point. And we believe we have successfully married a consulting system with writing expertise to clearly and beneficially present solutions to universal organizational challenges.

As we said above, this book is intended for any organization where there are two or more people working together. It will help everyone to understand and develop their leadership roles within the organization.

And remember — a leader is not necessarily only someone appointed or elected to a high position; a leader is someone who demonstrates leadership by example. This book is designed for the leaders in your organization, in your department, in your family, and in your community. The principles you will discover will be of immeasurable value in all of these environments.

You, and your organization, will become better focused. You will receive a "knowledge model" that will help you to plan and organize for success. You will discover greater results for all stakeholders — all the people who have a financial or personal investment in your organization. Your organization will have an enhanced performance level. And you and your fellow team members will discover a new level of fulfillment, of job satisfaction.

HOW TO USE THIS BOOK

Read it, a chapter at a time. At the end of each chapter you will find key notes and aids in the planning process. We encourage you to read each chapter, and then carry it — physically and ideologically — into your organization.

By bringing this into your organization, consider including as many of your staff as possible. The more involvement you develop as you work through this process, the faster the changes will occur and the sooner the alignment will improve. We will provide examples of situations concerning how to work through these processes in a team fashion.

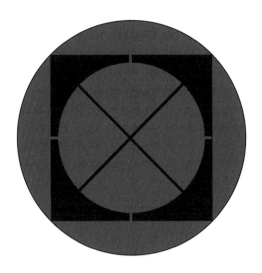

CHAPTER ONE
WHY ISN'T THIS WORKING ANY MORE?

"Holy cow, the road just disappeared!"

You slam on your brakes and sit shaking and sweating behind the wheel, with the car stopped only feet from the edge of a cliff. You had checked the map, and a road definitely was marked, and a cliff definitely was not! What the heck is going on?

That is the question at the top of the list for many business people in North America today. And the quick answer is that everything has changed, the roads are gone, and the maps are wrong. Business methods and concepts that have worked just fine — in fact, often better than fine — for decades, are now as useless as an outdated map.

In this chapter we want to focus on *CHANGE*. The change we will examine will include an overview analysis of our environment and a model that we will use to illustrate organizational alignment. Finally, we will explore the human dimension that presents the greatest challenges to effective change, namely our "paradigms". We will not go into each of these areas in detail, but will provide you with some food for thought on some of the changes affecting our world.

Historical overview of North American business

Our businesses, by and large, are built on a post-World War II model. The years following the Second World War were close to ideal for North American business. Everything was in our favour. North America was the number one supplier of goods and services to the entire free world, geared up for action because of war-time industry, and basically undamaged, unlike the business infrastructures of the devastated countries of Europe and the Far East.

The "success" of the war years set the pattern for post-war life in general. Our leaders were the same individuals who had led in war — and brought back with them a style of managing that worked well in war-like situations. With the advances in technology occasioned by the war, our assembly line process had been refined to a mature and reliable machine. From this evolved the leadership methods applied by the people who run our organizations.

We could churn it out, and the war-weary consumers — growing numbers of them, because of the post-war phenomenon known as the "baby boom" — gobbled it up.

Not unnaturally, we applied the post-war methods that were bringing business success to other aspects of life. This assembly line, cookie-cutter mentality was duplicated in our schools. It became an over-riding paradigm, setting the pattern for how we thought things should be, and how things worked best.

We are all familiar with certain rules that were enforced in every classroom of every school we attended. "Don't cheat" meant "don't talk to your neighbour; don't seek answers from your classmates." Today, one key to success in any organization is exactly the opposite: teamwork and cooperation— talking, consulting, collaborating with your neighbour. For most of us who are 25 years of age or older, this is a major, and often difficult, shift.

George Land in his book 'Grow or Die', identified three phases of growth that apply to all organizations — formative, normative and transformational.

The 'formative' phase occurs when organizations are trying to determine how to do things, such as the correct methods of production, and how to operate in an efficient manner.

In considering the formative phase relative to North American business, we can see this as representing the beginning phases of industrial development. From a historical perspective, this would represent the latter part of the 19th century and the first number of decades of the 20th century. During this time, most of the business development was in an experimental fashion in building the structures and systems that would operate in the most efficient manner. There was a great deal of discovery of processes that would serve us best, such as the assembly line, and figuring out the best way to produce the products and services demanded. Through trial and error, we built a very strong industrial machine that proved itself when the demand was highest, during World War II.

The *'normative'* phase occurs when the organization has clearly determined the most efficient manner of operation and has developed products that are producing results. In this phase, you "keep doing what you're doing". You don't alter anything, because things are working fine. This works well only in a stable environment, where change is not present.

The North American industrial society has spent almost four decades in the normative phase. After World War II the focus in North America was on production. If you think about the rest of the world, a large part was rebuilding from the destruction caused by the war. The Communist countries were going into seclusion (behind the Iron Curtain) and were not part of the rebuilding process, world-wide. That left North America to produce the good and services to rebuild. Up until the late 70s and early 80s, we did not feel any pressure from outside nations, but just had to focus on "producing". This is great if you want to keep succeeding in an unchanging environment; but it's disaster if the environment changes around you.

And change has become the definition of our world.

The *'transformational'* phase occurs when things start to break down; the old systems and processes are not working as well as in the past. In this phase, if an organization is to remain viable, it must rebuild the way it is operating and start anew.

The "re-engineering" that we are presently in the midst of reflects this transformational phase in operation. Organizations must change the entire way they are operating in order to survive and grow.

What changes have taken place to so challenge the fundamental concepts of North American business? There are many:

The rising expectations of the work force:

The North American worker has changed.

He and she are better educated, in many ways. Our workers have more formal education, and they are also accustomed to an incredible variety of informal educational opportunities, through the many forms of the media (television, the diverse world of advertising, newspapers, magazines, movies), through travel, and certainly through the general proliferation of information.

These highly-educated baby boomers are in the prime of their careers; hardly the sort of people to happily accept a career as a "cookie cutter". They want more, and they are exploring many ways and means to get more — more job satisfaction, more fulfilling leisure time, more control over their personal lives. This higher level of consciousness is resulting in a significant shift in what people want, both from their careers and from life in general.

The changes within our work environment:

The men who formed the bulk of the work force in the years following the war would not recognize the work place today. Everything has changed. Women have taken what should soon — hopefully — be an equal place in business. The advances in technology can barely be believed, even from our present-day perspective. Competition is ever more intense, in almost all fields. And business must cope with the increasing influence of government on business, especially in the areas of human rights, and "reporting" — the seemingly endless red tape that business must go through to be allowed, by government, to stay in business.

"Faster. Better. Cheaper" is becoming the trade mark of successful corporations in the market place today. Because of this "trade mark", organizations need to consider how they will be able to accommodate these three elements of change. This means that throughout each organization, all areas need to identify their part in adapting to a "Faster, Better, Cheaper" mentality. With this has come the need to specifically understand individual contributions to each organization's effectiveness and success.

The quality movement:

Quality has become a key focus in business today, and in areas beyond the immediately obvious. Quality is key because competition has increased in almost every area of business — there aren't many marketplaces dominated by a monopoly, these days — and buyers' expectations have increased dramatically. This has led to the need to continuously improve your products and services.

The Quality Movement means a fundamental change from how we have thought about business for 50 years. Cookie-cutter mentality does not co-exist well with a focus on improvement. Assembly-line thinking can be contradictory to an emphasis on service and continuous improvement.

And we must remember that quality cuts both ways. Managers have to realize that while we want our staff members to focus on quality of product and service, those staff members want the managers to offer improved quality of job satisfaction, and overall quality of life. We want quality to be on the minds of our employees as they enter the workplace; we must realize quality is also on their minds as they leave. Quality of life is an issue now very much on the minds of employees as they make decisions. This has a tremendous impact on business today.

The International Scene:

We all know the truth: our world has changed, is changing, and will continue to change.

The eastern block is dismantled and unstable; southeast Asia is a new and powerful player; new alliances are arising — in Europe, North America, even the mid-East. The Third World is keenly conscious of the relative prosperity and advantages in the First World; and all of these places, everywhere on the globe, are instantly accessible through modern communications, as the prophecy of the Global Village is more than realized. Competition has thus become a much more powerful and diverse factor than before.

Of course, business has always competed — but usually

with other businesses that worked in a similar environment. Today, the challenge is global, diverse and enormous.

So what? What does all of this mean?

It means that changes that are, at first, apparently external to our organizations must be reflected in internal changes — in organizational structure, in our management structures, and, in fact, in our managers and employees, resulting in a total change in how we go about doing business.

The methods that worked in the past won't work any more. Old-style business is simply not sustainable; we are living on borrowed time. Our organizations cannot succeed — in fact, cannot survive — unless we change our methods of operation.

This lesson has already been learned, to a large extent, in our educational systems. In this area, we have realized what needed to change, and if you have visited a school recently (and not only a university computer lab — a grade four classroom will do just as well) you know that a change has truly come.

In that classroom, you will find a lot that is not familiar to you — and may be different from yesterday, or tomorrow, because our education system has learned the necessity of flexibility. You will see four or five children sitting at a table, working together on a project, while another child is working by herself — for the moment. You will find joint projects, cooperation, consultation, and flexibility are the order of the day. You will find that the pupils often leave the classroom — to visit the library, or for an accompanied trip downtown, where they will have on-the-spot teaching about urban geography, for example.

You will find that learning by rote is almost a thing of the past, as are tests and exams — the focus is much more on learning to learn than it is on learning a specific set of facts. You will find that the children are comfortable with modern tools and technology — and also comfortable with the fact that these tools may change; that this month's computer may be next month's technological compost.

In other words, while there may be failures in the education system, it is focused on several objectives that are key to our children's success: learning to learn; flexibility; adaptability to change; and technology.

Compare for a minute the changes that have taken place in the classroom with the changes that have taken place in our corporate structures, especially in the way we work with our people.

It is instantly clear that we in the business world have a long way to go. The human asset area is the most difficult to change, and we have fallen a long way behind.

And the challenge here is, of course, that people — unlike machines on an assembly line — cannot be shut down and re-tooled in a weekend. You may be able to outfit your plant with new equipment, but the time and effort needed to re-align your people is a lot greater. But it's a lot more important, as well, because the best equipment in the world will not compensate for a failure to maximize your human assets.

Dr. Stephen R. Covey, author if *"The 7 Habits of Highly Effective People"*, has said "Every organization is perfectly aligned to get the results that it gets."

Remember, in the introduction to this book, our comparison with car alignment? Your car will operate precisely according to its alignment. If the wheels are set to run 15 degrees to the right, it will consistently perform in that manner. Some people actually get used to fighting the steering wheel all the time, to the point where they begin to forget that the car is not properly aligned to follow a straight line down the highway.

There are a lot of businesses and organizations that run like that car and driver. They are used to fighting an out-of-alignment structure, and it never occurs to them that alignment may be their corporate problem.

Any football player knows full well that if the members of the offensive squad are not aligned — if they do not share an understanding of the next play — then, no matter how well one or all perform on an individual basis, they are going to lose a lot of yardage.

If the quarterback executes a hand-off perfectly, but the half-back he wants to give the ball to is 20 yards down field, looking for a pass, the quarterback is probably going to end up on his back, on the turf, taking a big loss.

In business, if the manager believes that he has handed the responsibility for improved product to his employees, but they believe they should be operating at full tilt to produce more of the existing products, the business is probably headed for a loss.

Proper alignment is crucial.

Let's take a look at the big picture in business. There are a number of important elements that need to be managed for a business to operate in an efficient and effective manner. These include:

1) *The plant* — the bricks and mortar that house the assets or the organization.

2) *The processes* — how you get from the beginning of your business — products and services — to the end — your customer. One way of looking at process would be to imagine your business as an assembly line from beginning to end. All the things that happen along that assembly line are your processes.

By the way, today, the practice of re-engineering jobs is often considered to be part of process, because it is driven by the need for efficient operation. However, dealing with it exclusively in this category will probably produce very unhappy employees, despite your re-engineered systems and processes.

3) *Financial and legal matters* — an area that is of increasing importance in today's complex organizations and overall environment. This includes sourcing and managing incoming and outgoing investment, revenue and expenses, and overseeing legal arrangements ranging from patents to contract negotiations. It includes all financial aspects within your organization from cost of supplies to wages of employees to costs of goods and services.

4) *Products and services* — development of products and

services your organization will produce; positioning and market evaluation; the quality of your products and services and where they fit in the market.

5) *Marketing* — of products or services; how your prospective clients learn about what you do; and how you keep in touch with the needs and wants of your customers.

6) *Technology* — how technology is positioned, evaluated and utilized (or leveraged) represents a key aspect of the future success of most organizations today. Already today, to a large extent, how we utilize what technology can do for us is reflected in the current success — or lack thereof — of our organizations.

For many businesses, the list of present-day concerns might end here. But there is one other key element that must be considered:

7) *Leadership.* This begins at the senior levels of the corporation, but actually includes **everyone** in the organization. Companies that come to understand alignment, as applied to the entire corporate team, will find success much more easily.

This is the key to the choices and/or process we have for you in this book. We're going to look at leadership, and we are going to suggest a significant shift in how we manage in today's business world.

Effective Leadership

What do we mean by "effective"?

We have used the 'aligned car' example on a number of occasions and will do so again to illustrate what we mean by 'effective'. For a car to operate in an effective manner, there need to be a number of things in place: understanding the uses for the car, by everyone who will be affected by the car; knowing where you are going; having the right mechanical elements in place to operate the car; having the driver connected with how the car operates, the destination and why you are going to this destination; finally, all these areas must work in harmony one with another.

If we take each of the above examples, we can build what we mean by "effective":

- understanding the uses for the
  car, by everyone who will be
    affected by the car: NEEDS

- knowing where you are going: DIRECTION

- having the right mechanical
  elements in place to operate
  the car: SYSTEMS

- having the driver connected
  with how the car operates,
  the destination and why you
  are going to this destination: BEHAVIOUR

- all these areas must work in
  harmony one with another: ALIGNMENT

We will build upon these elements of 'effectiveness' as we develop the model to support 'effective leadership'.

What do we mean by "leadership"?

The word "leadership" immediately causes most employees to look up to the next level of their organization, and beyond. They may look up with respect and admiration, or with veiled disgust. But for them, that is where leadership lies — "up there."

Leadership means "taking responsibility". Taking responsibility in all aspects of what we will explore as we move together toward organizational alignment. In considering the above areas of NEEDS, DIRECTION, SYSTEMS, BEHAVIOUR AND ALIGNMENT, we will look at taking responsibility in your approach, working at understanding and incorporating each of these areas.

To build an effective company, you have to realize that everyone is a leader. Everyone in the company must take responsibility for the organization. Everyone must lead by functioning in an effective, focused manner, so the organization functions in an effective, focused manner.

An example of this way of thinking involves the concept of working as "champions" — team members throughout the organization who take personal initiative and have a personal investment in the coherent and creative progress of the organization; whose personal success aligns with the organizational success factors.

The old-fashioned idea of leader as the "guy or guys at the top" breaks down, in at least two ways. First, because it denies the leadership role of the majority of employees in any corporation. Second, because many of the supervisory people who would be considered leaders aren't providing any leadership, anyway. They may be managing people, but that doesn't mean they are leading people.

In effective corporations, everyone functions as a leader. Everyone takes responsibility for their role as part of the overall direction that the company is following. Everyone knows the goals of the company, and understands where they fit in. Each employee understands where his or her role fits into the big organizational picture — and what their specific contribution is to the maintenance and development of that picture. And when it is their turn to pass on that vision, they do so. That's leadership.

That may mean the CEO being sure his or her speech at the annual meeting accurately sets out the vision and direction of the company. Or it may mean the shipper on the loading dock, understanding that customer service is an element critical to success, and actually delivering a missed package in his own car. It will mean that the receptionist understands that her voice is the initial impression callers receive of the company, and that she is, as the vanguard of the company team, a leader in a very real sense. And it may mean that the vice president in charge of production looks for reward systems that do not pit team members against each other, but instead that encourage them to work together for the common good, allowing their mutual ideas to lead the entire organization to greater success.

It means managers spending the time with their team, being sure everyone is "on side", and heading in the same direction. It means that the days must be over when someone ignores a mistake, or tolerates poor service to a client, because "it's not my job." It means that the company has considered its compensation philosophy, so people are appropriately rewarded for doing their share — and more — in making their company's vision a reality.

This is shared, effective leadership. And it is absolutely central to success in the coming decades.

Organizational leadership effectiveness

Leadership effectiveness does not just happen; nor can it be developed quickly and left to function on its own.

Leadership effectiveness needs to be managed with as much care and attention as your actual product assembly line.

There are five specific areas which require attention if your organization is to develop effective, across-the-board leadership, and thus to operate effectively. They are:

1) Stakeholders:

Your stakeholders include all those who have an investment in the operation of your organization. Some are obvious — your clients, your employees, your management team. Others are less immediately evident — your suppliers, and the families of your employees, for example. To begin to develop organizational leadership effectiveness, you must develop a comprehensive list of all of your organization's stakeholders. You must then analyze and come to understand the needs/wants of your stakeholders. You must analyze how well your products/services are meeting their needs/wants.

2) Direction:

Your organization must develop, or re-capture, a clear

sense of direction. This will probably begin with a re-examination of the foundational direction of your organization — what was the vision that inspired its birth? From there, you will be concerned with long-term direction, and short-term, probably 12-month, direction. In other words, where were you going in the first place; where do you want to go from here; and what do you need to do in the next year to start moving down that long-term road.

3) Structures, Systems and Styles:

Because these elements, especially the first two, are much more apparent on a day-to-day basis than stakeholders or direction, many organizations tend to focus here when it becomes evident that there is a problem that needs to be solved. But these areas can be reformed or developed properly only on the basis of a proper understanding of the needs of your stakeholders, and a thorough grasp of the short- and long-term goals of your company. Only then can you begin to analyze and reform your structures, your systems and your styles.

4) People and Behaviour:

These key elements in your organizational equation come appropriately at this point — although, as we will see immediately below, this development is not linear and finite, but circular and ongoing. Too often, we believe our problems, and thus our solutions, arise from our people when, in fact, our people may be just fine, once we understand the needs of our stakeholders, our vision for the organization, and have established structures, systems and styles in concert with our new understanding.

It may be that we have an employee who will not become aligned to our organizational vision — but how will we know that until we have brought our organization into correct alignment? Apparent people problems often are not people problems at all — they are organizational weaknesses.

5) Alignment:

Alignment is the ongoing process of utilizing the four dimensions of organizational leadership. Alignment will produce cooperation and thus success among the individuals within the organization, as they become aligned with the organization's focus. Achieving alignment demands awareness of the daily need to reflect on the 'smoothness of operations' in all the areas of the organization.

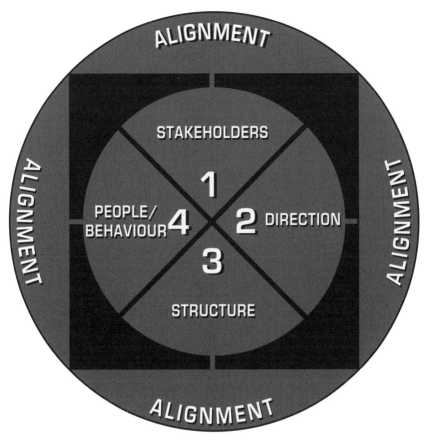

For illustration purposes, we have developed a circular management model, divided between these four equal elements. The reason we have chosen a circle is simple: it emphasizes that the job of managing and developing these elements is never complete — an effective company will lead from within this circle. It is an ongoing process, dynamic and sequential. The process requires alignment from number one through number four, and finding and maintaining a balance among all four which recognizes their mutual importance and inter-connectedness.

In considering the flow of these areas, we will briefly

describe each area and them examine each of them in detail in the remainder of the book.

The starting place, now, and in the future, is always with the **Stakeholders**. The following statement is baffling but true: most organizations ignore their stakeholders in their planning and development processes. And yet, this is the most obvious and essential starting place there can be!

We begin, then, with your Stakeholders. It is important to note that we analyze from the outside, in and fix from the inside, out. Our process allows this to happen.

A thorough understanding of your Stakeholders will enable you to proceed to set the Direction of your organization. Far too many organizations set their direction without careful consideration of their stakeholders' needs, and the organization's present level of performance.

That's a little like starting away from a stoplight with your car in third gear — it may go, but with minimal efficiency and maximum difficulty.

And the first thing in building leadership effectiveness is understanding and considering your Stakeholders. Then you can effectively establish Direction.

Only after **Direction** is set — including re-examination of your organization's initial vision, and the establishment of long-term and short-term directional goals (this is similar to articulating your corporate vision) — is it time to develop **Structures, Systems and Styles**.

You can see that many organizations are driven almost

entirely by this third element on the wheel, while the corporation has long since lost touch with its stakeholders and its sense of corporate direction. Or even if the folks in the boardroom understand the direction, the people actually delivering the service are not sharing that vision.

That is where **People and Behaviour** becomes an important element — and, as you will see, those people are on your Stakeholders' list, which takes you back on your second swing around the wheel.

Alignment encircles the above four areas. It is a continuous, ongoing process of understanding and bringing people on board with regard to each area. For example, understanding the stakeholder needs, clarity in direction, working within the structures and systems that support organizational direction, and behaving in a manner consistent with the values and mission of the organization. Another way to say that is to suggest that your people need to share common paradigms on needs, direction, structures and systems and behaviour.

Paradigms:

We have used the word "paradigm" more than once already. Let's be sure we understand what it means. Paradigms are personal, internal road maps, the rules and regulations, our basic assumptions, and how we visualize our roles. These paradigms act as internal guiding mechanisms in our interpretation of our life events, and in directing our efforts and focus.

Today's world calls for a lot of paradigm shifting. That can be tough — paradigms are, by their very nature, built into our way of approaching life, and we are largely unaware of them until we call them out of our subconscious for objective evaluation. Yet your paradigms govern your actions and interactions, every day.

For example, when you meet someone for the first time, how do you evaluate them? On objective, factual knowledge you have about them? No, because you don't have that information, yet. Instead, you evaluate them on their appearance, their age, their sex, their race, their clothing — as you compare and evaluate the information gathered in those categories with your built-in sense of what is best and what is bad, what is comfortable and what is odd — with your paradigms, your set of assumptions.

We operate at all times using our own collection of paradigms in every area of life. We therefore see the world not as it is, but by how we view things.

And it is easy to see, given the impact of paradigms on how we act and react, the danger presented by wrong, inappropriate, or outdated paradigms.

CHAPTER ONE: KEY NOTE REVIEW

• Efficiency and Effectiveness must be developed within these component parts of organizations:
  • The Plant
  • The Processes
  • Financial and Legal matters
  • Products and Services
  • Marketing
  • Technology
  • Leadership

These segments represent the major asset areas of any organization: physical, financial, technological and human.

• Organizational Leadership Effectiveness depends on balance and alignment in the following areas:
  • Stakeholders' needs and wants
  • Direction and strategy of the organization
  • Structures, systems and styles of operations
  • People and behaviour of all internal stakeholders
  • **Alignment within and among the above areas**

• Paradigms are our internal 'road maps' — basic assumptions, rules and regulations, and the criteria that we subconsciously bring to our actions and decision-making in every area of life.

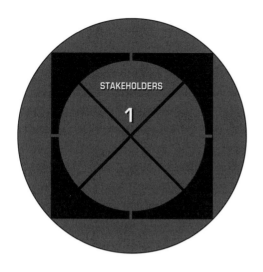

CHAPTER TWO
STAKEHOLDERS

For whom are you operating your organization?

That is a basic question that often gets bypassed, at full speed, in the everyday rush to accomplish everyday tasks. But a moment of reflection — say, right now — will quickly lead you to the conclusion that this is a very fundamental question.

We are talking about stakeholders. And we will consider three key questions concerning your stakeholders:

Who are your stakeholders?

What are the needs and wants of your stakeholders?

How are you doing in meeting those needs and wants?

First, a definition:

Simply put, stakeholders are individuals or groups of people who are affected by, or affect, your organization. A typical list of stakeholders will include customers, employees, owners, and suppliers. It may also include a number of other stakeholders — we'll mention a few later on — but this is a core list of stakeholders that probably applies to most organizations.

Let's think about these groups for a moment.

Customers are the people to whom you sell or deliver your products or services. Almost any organization, these days, will describe itself as customer-driven. But ask yourself: at month-end, are you evaluating your successes and failures in customer service, or are you considering only the financial bottom line? Being up to date on your financial state is obviously a good idea, but if that is all you are measuring, you may not be as customer-focused as you believe.

In fact, when considering your customer, think about the following questions:

• Who are your customers today?

• Who should be your customers today?

• Who will be or may be your customers in the future?

- How will your customer base change in the future?

- How soon will that occur?

Employees are obviously crucial to the success of any organization. But again, it is a rare organization that consistently measures or even discusses successes or failures in this area.

It is not that rare that organizations operate something like this: they call a meeting of their employees. "Listen, you guys," they say, "We want you to understand this very clearly. Our customers are the reason we exist. We're going to treat them with respect and consideration. We're going to drive this through your thick skulls until you get it right! You can be replaced, you know. So get customer-focused, treat them right, treat them with respect!"

Sure. That's right up there with the parent who says, "Damn it, Johnny, I told you not to swear!" Your organization will find it very difficult to encourage employees to be customer-focused, if your managers are not employee-focused.

Owners are usually the first — and often the only — stakeholders on an organizational list. And the needs and wants of your organization's owners must be heeded. Identifying those needs and wants, understanding them, and focusing on them, at the same time as you are considering the needs and wants of other stakeholders, will help your organization to thrive. For example, a typical need of owners is for profit. That's understandable. Meeting the needs and wants of customers and employees should be the fast track to that goal.

Owners may be ignored by organizations, as well, especially if a complex corporate chart removes the organization a lengthy administrative distance from the owners. Some organizations have become so customer-driven, or even employee-driven, that absentee owners suddenly discover their needs and wants have been relegated to last place. That is not good business, and it is also not conducive to long-term managerial job security.

Suppliers should be on your "A" list of stakeholders. Often, suppliers are looked on as being outside of the loop, but they really should be on the inside. Today, we're finding more and more organizations looking at closer relationships with suppliers. In some cases, they are approaching their relationship like a partnership.

This is 180 degrees from what has happened in the past, when the relationship with suppliers was actually adversarial. Wal-Mart guru Sam Walton was one of the first to implement a new approach, seeking to learn the needs of his supplying partners. For example, he could negotiate lower prices from suppliers if he took care of the shipping, himself. He actually financed the suppliers at times, again enabling Wal-Mart to reduce wholesale prices. Walton's partnership with his suppliers gave him pricing advantages over competitors who were working with the same suppliers!

Customers. Employees. Owners. Suppliers. These will be on almost every list of stakeholders. But think beyond them, and inside them.

Beyond them you may find other stakeholders, such as family members. Perhaps your organization expects its employees to travel a lot; what needs and wants does that create for their families? Should you consider those family members as stakeholders? Many organizations now do. Some include government as a stakeholder, because of the need for constant reporting and, in many cases, financial accountability.

Inside the first four groups you may find sub-groups with individual needs and wants. For example, a restaurant chain with franchisees will want to consider the franchise owners as one customer stakeholder group, and the people who eat in the restaurants as another.

As well, when you consider employees as stakeholders, it will probably be true that certain groups of your employees have very different needs and wants compared to other groups. Senior managers and receptionists, for example, may have common areas, but they will probably show some very different needs, as well.

Why start your organizational analysis with stakeholders?

You start here because in coming to genuinely and thoroughly understand your stakeholders, and their needs and wants, you will identify your organization's reason for being. You will answer the question, "Why does this organization exist?"

The stakeholder analysis not only illustrates the need for your organization, but it will also pin-point the problem areas. If you do your analysis thoroughly, you will know exactly which stakeholder needs are being met, and which are not.

Step one is **identifying your stakeholders.** We have

already suggested some of the individuals and groups that will be on your list: Customers, employees, owners, suppliers. We've suggested that you move beyond and inside these groups, and be sure you have a complete answer to the question: *who do we affect, and who affects us?*

Clarity in understanding who your stakeholders are puts in front of you the groups of individuals who are within your organizational world, and without whom you would have no world. Consider this: if any of these primary stakeholder groups were not part of your world, would your world exist at all? This should illustrate the importance of knowing your stakeholders.

We suggest that you also ask, after that first exercise: *Who will be our stakeholders of the future, in five years, or ten years?* This helps you to avoid structuring your organization to meet current needs, while ignoring the peril of obsolescence. For example, an organization in the publishing business must consider current readers, but will perish unless it is keenly aware of the need to attract new readers in the future. Those future stakeholders may have very different needs and wants than current readers; understanding their needs and wants will greatly help the publisher to plan for future success.

Such an approach may mean that the organization needs to consider future suppliers, as well. To continue with the publishing example, it may be that bitter competitors — cable TV companies, for example — will have to become allies in the business of providing information. This is not a prophecy, mind you, simply an example of where identifying future stakeholders may lead.

Step Two is **answering the question, "What are the needs and wants of your stakeholders?"**

Do not take this question for granted. And do not assume that you, or anyone in your organization, knows the answer. It is very probable that no one in your organization has ever done this exercise, or has ever even thought in these terms.

We know of a large, sophisticated company that has a large, sophisticated marketing plan. It's really a book, more than 50 pages long.

What should be at the heart of that marketing plan? The obvious answer is, an analysis of the needs of the customers.

Have they done that? When asked that question, their senior vice president said, "That's a heck of a good question. No, I guess we haven't."

Why? Because they haven't focused on their customers' (stakeholders') needs, just on the products they could sell them. They are numbers-driven, focusing on the bottom line, but not fully clued in to how one optimizes that bottom line. They're ready to market to clients, but they have never asked the clients what they want. That seems highly inefficient, at best; a recipe for unemployment, at worst.

This kind of short-circuit thinking arises from two problems. First, the problem of assuming. We assume we know the answer. We assume someone else has done the background work. We assume that if the customer wanted that service last year (he bought it, didn't he?), he'll want it again this year.

Second, the problem of quick fixes. We have come through a business era of the quick fix. There were dozens of methods to fix your problems, overnight. Some of them actually brought short-term solutions.

But putting a new coat of paint on your house to disguise the fact that termites are chewing it to the ground really doesn't solve anything, long term. You will look better for a little while; then everything will collapse.

Someone once asked Albert Einstein what he would do if he were presented with a problem, and an hour in which to solve it. He said he would take 55 minutes to analyze the problem, and five minutes to formulate the solution.

Stakeholder analysis is part of the 55-minute drill. There are no apparent, immediate results. You would look better, as the decision maker, if you got the painters painting immediately, instead of bringing in the pest control experts to do a study of termite infestation.

But which approach would leave you ahead of the game, five years from now?

A lot of people have found a comfortable job description inside their organizations: they are firefighters. They run around, putting out fires, getting adrenaline boosts from solving problems and producing product. They fall asleep in planning sessions, so they avoid them.

Avoiding analysis and planning is avoiding success.

How do you go about identifying the needs and wants of

your stakeholders?

Ask them.

Ask your customers. Ask your employees. Ask your own-ers. Ask your suppliers. (There are some sample question-naires at the end of this chapter which will help you understand the methods best used to obtain honest and useful information.)

Avoid third-party information. Do not, for example, ask your sales representatives about the needs and wants of your customers. That may only perpetuate some problems that you are trying to solve. Don't ask your managers to identify the needs and wants of your employees.

We're not assuming dishonesty, just a lack of under-standing. You may be astonished at the things that are important to your employees. Companies have discovered to their shock that flexible time was more important than paycheques; that an extra week of holidays was rated higher than a raise worth three weeks' salary; that employees are genuinely interested in understanding what is really going on within the organization; and that they want to be asked for their ideas on how to do things better.

With your employees, you may want to hold brainstorm-ing sessions, to gain their thoughts and ideas concerning the important needs and wants of all stakeholder groups. (The brainstorming process is explained in the review notes to this chapter). Make lists of the needs and wants, and then prioritize them. Many companies can accom-plish this as an entirely internal exercise.

On the other hand, some may realize that there are large internal problems with trust and communication, and that is where an outside facilitator may be necessary, if you are to arrive at honest and comprehensive answers.

Outside involvement is probably not necessary with owners, and with suppliers. The owner is probably the person driving this exercise, and therefore there will be no hidden agenda or lack of trust to block an accurate assessment of the owner's needs and wants. The owner will be only too happy to communicate these things with his or her organization.

Suppliers should present few problems, as well, since they are probably interested in telling you the truth, because you are their customer, and they want the relationship to work.

An outside facilitator may be of help in working with customers, and with employees. Customers are very interested in having their needs met, but this does not mean that they will be entirely open — there is a long-standing tradition of keeping up your guard when you are facing someone who wants to sell you something. An impartial third party may be able to help, here. But many companies will want to approach the customers directly, and will successfully use this opportunity to build on the relationships, as well as to identify the needs of this particular stakeholder group.

Customers and suppliers can be approached through questionnaires, focus groups, and conversations with members of your team. Again, do everything practical to ensure that you are getting honest and comprehensive answers.

Here is a simple format to use in identifying the needs of your customers. Ask them:

What do you like about what we're doing right now?

What are we not doing right now that you would like us to do?

What are we doing right now that you don't like?

Is there anything else that we haven't talked about that you think is important, that we should talk about?

These questions can also be a good starting point with suppliers and with employees.

In many organizations, the employee needs analysis is the area most filled with pitfalls; here, some companies find an outsider essential. Again, others, working from a more solid foundation of trust and communication, find this to be an exciting and profitable process, carried out entirely independently.

In all cases, resist the temptation to become warm and fuzzy. Almost every organization — certainly every one in the business sector — exists to make a profit, and will not exist if that goal is not reached. Therefore, it is dishonest and unhelpful if the needs of the owners — and perhaps the employees, as well — do not include a prominent reference to financial success.

It may sound more pleasant if the corporate needs are to have happy employees and happy customers, but excluding financial success as an important need, as well, devalues this entire analysis.

In the same way, if there are expressed needs — more likely, wants — that your organization is not going to be able to meet (six weeks' vacation for all employees; 75% cost reduction to customers), then say so. Don't appear to make commitments that cannot be kept; the key to this exercise is honesty and dealing with reality, both when gathering the information and when giving feedback.

Okay. You have gathered the lists of needs and wants from your organization's various stakeholders. Now what?

Step three will include **prioritizing the needs and wants and evaluating your present level of performance.**

Decide which needs and wants demand immediate attention. We strongly encourage organizations to limit the number of needs to be addressed to a manageable amount.

There is no magic number, but if you are past five and approaching ten key needs of a specific stakeholder group, you are probably on the far edge of practicality.

Then, with the final lists made, evaluate how well your organization is doing in meeting those needs. A simple and understandable method is to rate your performance on a scale of 1 to 10. (10 equals excellent, 8 equals good, 5 equals okay, 3 equals poor, and one equals needle in the eye).

We encourage you to evaluate the areas as an internal, organizational exercise, and also to ask your stakeholders to evaluate your organizational performance in these areas.

For example: the employees say one of their needs is for decent working conditions. Ask them how they rate the present conditions on a scale of 1 to 10. They want flexible time. Ask them to rate the present situation.

If the majority of employees feel their working conditions are around an 8, but the organization's provision of flex-time is a 2, then you have instantly identified an area for attention. However, it may be impossible for your organization to offer flex-time, even though it is apparently important to your employees. So tell them the truth.

In all cases, it is essential that the organization's conclusions and directions be communicated to the stakeholder groups involved. You may be able to explore alternatives together; at the least, honest communication always builds a better foundation.

Step four is **evaluating the other important areas of the organization that need to be well-managed.**

To gain a complete overview of your organizational health, it is good to rate your performance in five other areas, as well. Adding this analysis to your stakeholder findings will tell you exactly where you are, and what you need to change to bring your organization into alignment.

Rate on a scale of one to ten:

How is our plant and process operating today?

If your machinery is obsolete or poorly maintained, then happy employees will not necessarily solve your impending production problems. However, brand-new, glitch-free machines are worthless if you have unmotivated, mis-aligned employees.

Today we are hearing a great deal about "re-engineering" within organizations. One aspect of re-engineering relates to evaluating the processes and systems that are presently in place within an organization, and fine-tuning or improving the efficiency and effectiveness of these processes. This represents an important aspect of adapting an organization to meet the market needs, and is an important evaluation process. Certainly, "process evaluation" needs to precede any structural changes you may be considering!

Where are we financially?

For most companies, analyzing this particular component is as natural as breathing — it's the other areas, especially stakeholder analysis, that needs to be a learned skill. However, do the financials we have provide the information we need to know to manage the business,

How good are our products and services?

Key answers to this question will arise from the stakeholder analysis of your customers' needs. However, there clearly needs to be daily attention in this area, as well.

How well are we doing at marketing?

Do you have a plan; is it aligned with what your customers have told you they want; is it being implemented; is the success monitored and evaluated effectively; how aware are you of the needs of your marketplace?

Where are we in technology?

How well are we using technology? How complete and on-target is our future planning when it comes to technology?

Rate your company, one to ten, in these five areas, as well as in the area of stakeholder needs. This will give you the big picture as to how your organization is presently performing.

Lots of people love to look at the big picture. They despise detail, and they revel in grand planning. They have believed for years that they truly can grasp the overview.

Dangerous relationship between overview and oversight

But there is a dangerous relationship between overview and oversight. Looking only at the grand scheme can leave you oblivious to the specific problems, the details that are being overlooked. The stakeholder analysis brings those details into sharp focus, and then allows you to develop an infinitely more accurate overview of the big picture.

You will probably find that your big picture looks more like an unfinished crossword puzzle than it does like a completed masterpiece. That is okay — now you know where the holes are, and what you need to do to fill them.

You may have discovered a marked lack of training, although your employees have said that opportunities for growth are important, and your customers have told you that their sales representatives don't seem to understand their needs. Now, you can move to solve that problem, meet the needs of stakeholders, and improve your organization's performance.

What you will end up with is — no surprise, here — better alignment. Your people will be headed in the same direction as your organization; you'll understand one another better; and you will have common goals. You'll have solved at least some of the problems that were roadblocks to understanding why your organization exists.

You must understand, here, that this process must be repeated on a regular basis. This is necessary for several reasons: because of the incredible rate of change in our world; because you have made a commitment to communicate with your stakeholders; because you don't want to get out of alignment, again.

You will need to set up mechanisms and methods to ensure accurate analysis of your stakeholder groups on an ongoing basis — regular questionnaires, perhaps, or focus groups. Whatever methods you use, the key is communication. You must communicate, honestly — it will enable you to identify problem areas. It will also engender loyalty, relationship-building, even a sense of ownership between the organization and its stakeholders.

In other words, in our ongoing organizational planning process, this stakeholder analysis must remain front and centre.

Let's say, for example, that last year, you asked your employees how they like working here. They gave it 3 out of 10. You talked to them, found out what they disliked, and now you must ask again. If they say 6 out of 10, you've made a start, but you have a way to go. If they say 3, again, you need to take another hard look at employee working conditions and employee relations in general.

What you must not do, this year, is assume you solved the problem raised last year, without asking the people who identified the problem.

This principle applies across the board. If your financial performance is a 2, you have to take action; if your technology is anywhere under 5, you have a problem to solve. Everything must be aligned, balanced, moving your organization ahead in the right direction.

When everyone in your organization is moving in the same direction, everyone can begin to act as a leader. Leadership requires confidence, a confidence that the leader knows the direction in which to go. You are now supplying that confidence to all your people.

If your employees understand the needs of your customers — identified through the stakeholder analysis — they can take responsibility for helping to meet those needs. That's leadership. If they understand the needs of suppliers, of the owner, the same holds true.

Here is a good exercise to help you assess your understanding of the needs of your stakeholders. After you have examined their needs and wants, develop an ideal statement of what you would want that stakeholder group to say about you as an organization.

Approach it this way: "We would want our customers to say this; we would want our employees to say this; we would want our owners to say this."

This is another way to focus on their needs, and how you're doing at meeting them. If you can write the statement with confidence, you understand their needs. If you can say the statement is true, today, you're in great shape. If not, you have another guide as to where you need to be going, concerning your stakeholders.

CHAPTER TWO: KEY NOTE REVIEW

• Customers, Employees, Owners, Suppliers — In each case use questions to gain a better understanding of their needs and wants.

Stakeholder Analysis Process

Step One: Stakeholder identification
Step Two: Stakeholder needs and wants
Step Three: Evaluation of present levels of performance
Step Four: Evaluation of other major areas of your
         organization.

Common Questions to all Stakeholders:

- What are we doing that you like?
- What are we not doing that you would like to see done?
- What are we doing that you don't like?
- What other areas might we consider doing for you that would be of benefit to you?

In addition to the above questions, which are useful for all groups, the following questions are specific to Customers and Employees.

Customer Needs and Wants Questions:

- Do you receive our products/services in the time expected?
- Is the quality of our products/services in line with your expectations?
- Is 'value' an important consideration for you in the products/services you purchase.
- Are the products/services delivered to you in a 'respectful' and caring fashion'?

Employee Needs and Wants Questions:

- Do you receive the right amount of direction concerning your job and concerning where the organization is going?
- Are you in a position where you 'own' your job?
- Do you know what 'success' means in your job?
- What specific areas or items would you need to better equip you to perform your job?
- Do you receive feedback and support that keeps you informed on how well you are doing and answers questions that you may have on how to do things better?

• **Evaluate each Stakeholder group by considering:**
  - What are their needs and wants related to your organization?
  - How well are you doing in meeting these needs and wants?
  - What may be the needs and wants (or how may

they change) of our stakeholders in the future?
- Who may be new stakeholders in the future?

• **Evaluate these major areas of your organization:**
  - Plant and Process operations
  - Financials
  - Products and Services
  - Marketing efforts
  - Technology and how effectively you are using it.

Brainstorming process:

Step # 1: Identify the area that you wish to explore (example: the primary needs of our customers)

Step # 2: Challenge the group to identify all the ideas that come to mind (all the ideas that come to mind for customers).

Step #3: Discuss and clarify what is meant by each of the needs identified or listed (example: what is meant by respect?)

Step #4: Consolidate into the most important areas.

CHAPTER THREE
DIRECTION

Setting your direction is possible only after you understand your organization's needs.

This is obvious, if you think about it for a minute. Imagine your spouse saying, "We need some..." and you leave the house at that moment, climb into your car, and set off to... where? You would have been smart to stick around long enough to hear the rest of the sentence: "We need some laundry detergent," "We need some milk," or "We need some peace and quiet around here!" would have probably sent you in very different directions.

We need to understand the needs of our stakeholders, and of our organizations, before we set direction.

Too often, organizations are heading in an entirely accidental direction — they're going somewhere, all right, but they have never taken the time to understand what the right direction for their organization is.

They may do a very fine job of finding and purchasing milk, but it does very little good when the need is for clean laundry.

There are three component parts of organizational direction, and they need to be explored and established in this specific order:

1) What is your foundation?

2) What is your vision (future picture)?

3) What are today's issues (and resulting goals and strategies)?

What is your foundation?

What is non-changing about your organization? Your values and beliefs. Your mission or purpose. Your management principles. Your Key Result Areas. These are your foundation. And this foundation includes the reason you exist, and the underpinnings of how you operate.

Your values and beliefs lie at the core of what you are, and how you operate. They are different from policies and procedures, which can change to meeting changing needs.

Values and beliefs are unlikely to change, unless in your evaluation process you discover some that are clearly detrimental, such as an underlying dishonesty or lack of respect in dealing with certain groups of employees. Even then, the odds are that the stakeholders of your organization have basic values that are contrary to those practices, and what you are looking at is changing dishonest or prejudicial procedures to bring them in line with foundational principles of honesty and respect.

What is your vision ?

Where are you going from here?

Where do you see yourselves in the future?

What is your potential?

You have looked at the needs of your stakeholders. Establishing your vision means developing a plan for the future that meets those needs, but it means more than that, as well — it means thinking creatively, putting yourself into the future picture, setting goals that include future stakeholders and incorporate the growth potential your aligned and focused organization has.

Imagine your company as a house. Your stakeholders are the people who relate to that house — the landlord, the occupants, the cleaning people, the newspaper delivery person, the neighbours. Now, look into the future — is this house large enough and designed properly to meet not only the present needs, but also the future needs of these stakeholders?

Most of us know someone who has a carefully planned family, who buys a car just right for a family of that size, and then who discovers that they are unexpectedly expecting another child. The new car no longer meets the needs of the family, or will not, in the very near future.

The unexpected means that no organization will have a perfect record of future planning. But taking time to establish your vision, and incorporating the potential for the unexpected — in general and then in detail — will help make sure the organization is properly designed for the future.

You need to look at the potential, even if you are not going to finish the house, right now. What may be part of this future picture?

What are today's issues?

Too many organizations focus only on what they see as today's issues. They are caught up in what has been wisely called the tyranny of the urgent.

The truth is, today's issues can only be properly addressed from a foundational understanding of your organization's vision for the future. Because you need to be setting policy, procedures and direction today that will efficiently and effectively carry your organization toward that successful future picture.

Your goals and strategies — which are the issues for today — come from understanding your future picture. From understanding where you're going. From understanding what the foundation is. From understanding how well you are doing right now. From understanding the needs of the stakeholders, and how well you are doing in meeting those needs.

Returning to the house analogy, 'today's issues' represent all the most important areas that need to be worked on, to work towards the future framework of the house, and address any shortfalls or areas of improvement needed throughout the house.

Here's how it works:

If this sounds unfamiliar, this is probably because far too many organizations allow their goals and strategies to arise from immediate needs that have no relationship to an organizational vision. They're often going around in circles.

Let's get off the merry-go-round, and set some effective direction. In the next three chapters, we will examine, in detail, your foundation, your vision, and today's issues for your organization. We will provide a process for you to follow, and the questions that will obtain the answers needed in creating your direction.

CHAPTER THREE: KEY NOTE REVIEW

• There are three component parts to direction: *foundation; vision* (or future picture of the organization); and *today's issues* and the goals and strategies that come from them.

CHAPTER FOUR
THE FOUNDATION

Your foundation is built of those things which are unchanging about your organization.

It is probably a good idea to qualify this right off the top: does this mean that your mission will never, ever change, or that your values will never change? Not necessarily — even these foundational elements may change, from time to time, and that's okay. Your organization is continually evolving, and there may be occasional, foundational alterations.

In considering the foundation, we will, however, be looking at those things that are the least likely to change about your organization. For example, your values and beliefs may evolve over time, but changing your fundamental values — honesty is out, dishonesty is in, for example — is going to confuse your stakeholders.

That may seem a ridiculous example, but if you have stressed honesty with your sales representatives, and suddenly tell them that it's okay to wildly exaggerate the benefits of your product, you will have very confused sales reps.

In this chapter, we're going to consider four elements of your foundation. One we've already mentioned: **values and beliefs**.

Then, we will look at the development of an organizational **mission statement**.

Third, we will consider **management principles**.

And then, we will talk about **Key Result Areas (KRAs)**.

Add these four issues together. What we are really asking is, "what do you want to be when you grow up?" or, "What is the nature of your being?"

Values and beliefs:

It is important to understand that you are not creating something new, here: your organization already has a value system in place, right now. You are not operating in a value and belief void.

However, it is very probable that your organization has neither examined nor articulated those values and beliefs, and therefore, many of your corporate practices are not aligned with them. This leads, immediately, to many of your employees operating out of alignment, as well.

In this section, we will help you to think through your values and beliefs. What are your values, right now? What do you want them to be?

Why do we start this foundation section with values and beliefs? For two reasons: First, it's the core. Your values and beliefs are at the centre of everything.

Second, because when you have arrived at a clear understanding of your organization's values and beliefs, this provides an essential foundation, and an ethical touchstone, for the development of your mission statement, and of your management principles.

If you do not understand and follow your organization's values and beliefs, you have a lack of alignment. Your managers and employees will be unsure as to what is foundational to your organization. There will be high degrees of inconsistency in the behaviours within your organization.

Values will give a foundation for decision-making, especially in the tough, ethical areas.

Setting out your organizational values and beliefs is a very serious business, because you are really setting up benchmarks, and you are inviting all of your stakeholders to compare your performance and your decisions with those benchmarks.

If you value honesty, then you really must be ready for a challenge from a sales rep who is encouraged to inflate the worth of the product in his or her sales pitch. And you had better be honest in the information you give to employees in staff meetings. If you value respect for people, this has to be practiced, not only toward your customers, but toward your employees. If you say you value innovation and creativity, then you should be prepared to allow the kind of work environment that encourages this.

As you articulate your values and beliefs, you need to look at two things: What are they, now? And, What do we want them to be?

We suspect the two lists will not be very different. What will be open for change will be the way that you apply the values and beliefs once they are openly and widely understood among our stakeholders.

You may conclude that "respect for people" is an important value of your organization. Good. Now, ask, "How does this apply to all of our stakeholders?"

Perhaps you have stressed respect for customers. Now, you will realize that if your organization is to be properly aligned, this must also apply to employees, and to suppliers. You will want to be inclusive of all appropriate stakeholder groups in your statement of values and beliefs. Don't say, "We will show respect to customers"; say, "We will show respect to everyone who comes in contact with this organization."

Some of your stated values and beliefs will be universals: honesty, integrity, respect, for example. Some may be more specific to your organization, such as valuing intrapreneurship, or teamwork.

When you are listing your values and beliefs, define what you mean by each one. If you list "teamwork", what does that mean? Do you mean friendly and respectful attitudes on the assembly line, where each worker does his or her own job; or do you mean an atmosphere of interaction, where employees meet together to brainstorm on problems or product development? Either is admirable, but be sure everyone is clear about what your values truly are.

Again, in this process, be brutally frank. It is no good saying "honesty" if you know you're not going to put it into practice, across the board. It is no good saying, "respect for people," if you want your employees to respect customers and managers but if managers aren't going to respect employees. Tell the truth about where you really want to live, in terms of values and beliefs.

Tremendous benefits arise from this exercise.

The first benefit is alignment. Many, many organizations are living in the dilemma that their practices — in general, or specifically — are not in alignment with their unstated values and beliefs. This causes innumerable problems, from poor interpersonal relationships, internally and externally, to impossible situations when it comes to employee discipline. It's hard to reprimand for behaviour that contradicts an unwritten code! The documentation is sadly lacking.

The second benefit relates to decision-making. Our values and beliefs provide a foundation on which to stand to make many of the key decisions that face us. Sometimes, we have made a decision, and we're now very uncomfortable with it. Often we will find that this is because it has gone against our underlying values. But unless we clearly understand those values, this will happen, again and again. Once we have a clear statement of values and beliefs, key decisions can be built on them.

But let's be honest: there may be conflict in values. As in anything you do, subjectivity comes into play, and you also need to recognize that. You are, after all, building human organizations with human strengths and weaknesses.

A third benefit is that an honest statement of values and beliefs will help all stakeholders decide if they can operate in alignment with those values and beliefs; if not, they will have some important decisions to make.

For example, let's talk about money. One of the real challenges in business is that organizations value money, they value money highly, but they are uncomfortable admitting this.

A business is well advised to state that one of its corporate values is profit. Managers and employees need to understand this. Now, if other values include integrity and respect for people, then you have a good, well-balanced foundation for an organization that will value its people, tell the truth, and still aim for a solid profit each year, which should guarantee employment for its staff and quality products for its customers.

If your values and beliefs make no mention of financial results, your stakeholders will have every right to wonder why, if you don't value money, financial results are among the most important reports, every meeting? There goes your integrity and honesty! Better to set out an honest list of values and beliefs, straight off.

Do not try to fool yourself with warm and fuzzy statements; do not duck the reality of the importance of financial success, or you will be instantly out of alignment, and your published list of values and beliefs will receive exactly the respect it deserves.

Another benefit is that stated values and beliefs provides, not only a foundation, but also a springboard for change. Organizationally and individually, you can compare your actions and decisions against the foundational beliefs, and correct yourself when you are going against them.

This really is a lot like the religious idea of repentance. The root meaning of the word repent is "to go in another direction". This is not a mystical concept — it simply means stop what you're doing, and do something else.

Our organizational values and beliefs will be signposts to point out that we're going down the wrong road, and we need to change direction.

Finally: stated values and beliefs will help enormously in the ongoing challenge that faces every for-profit organization: the conundrum of doing good while also achieving economic security.

Any business worth its salt wants to make money; that's achieving economic security. But any business with integrity also wants to do what is right.

Sometimes, it is a tough balancing act. If you over-emphasize doing good, you can change from a business to a charity to a bankruptcy case. If you over-emphasize economic security, you can sacrifice integrity and corporate image, and end up in exactly the same place.

Having a clearly stated set of values and beliefs will help you maintain that balance.

Once upon a time, a man bought a restaurant known far and wide for its homemade soup. People lined up at lunch time for a bowl of that soup. The restaurant made a reasonable profit, although the ingredients for the soup were expensive.

The new owner realized that he could make even more money by watering the soup, just a little. And he was right — for a few months, profits soared, because he had cut costs and maintained market share. For a few months.

You can guess the end of the story. The owner had forgotten the balancing act — he had opted for profit (not a bad thing, in balance), but he had forgotten the balance of doing the right thing. He short-changed a key group of stakeholders, and it cost him the business.

If that new owner had sat down and listed values and beliefs, including "integrity" and "full value to our customers", for example, he would have known he was taking his business out of alignment, and into receivership.

Setting out your values and beliefs, clearly defined, and with a definite commitment to adhering to those values and beliefs, is an important step on the road to an aligned, successful company.

Once you have a written statement of values and beliefs, you can proceed to the next building block of your organizational foundation: your **mission statement**.

A mission statement defines why your organization exists.

It is useful for a number of reasons: it is a reminder, during the formulation process and from then on, of the fundamental reason your organization came into being, and continues to be.

It is an important statement to your stakeholders. Internally, employees, managers and owners are reminded of what it takes for them to be aligned with the reason for being of the organization. Externally, stakeholders such as customers and suppliers are given a clear statement of what your organization is about.

Therefore, your mission statement needs to relate to, and have meaning for, all of your stakeholders. It also needs to incorporate the vision for the future that you have just arrived at; it needs to be challenging. Your mission statement should be something you can live by today, and that will also be meaningful and challenging tomorrow.

Elements of your mission statement will include a statement of the end result of your organization's efforts, and statements about the means your organization will use to accomplish those efforts.

Bear in mind that, since you have already completed a statement of values and beliefs, you will be able to reduce the length of your mission statement to something fairly simple, and very direct (we include some mission statements as examples at the end of this chapter). Your key document will also include your values and beliefs, so you do not need to state them again here.

As you look at your desired end result, and at your means to that end, you will realize that they must be compatible.

As you begin to prepare your mission statement, you will want to seek the input of as many of your employees as possible. The people in your organization need to feel that they are a part of this process.

How this works out, in practical terms, depends on your organization. If you have a staff of 12, it may be possible to work together from start to finish. If you have 200 or 20,000, this may be tougher. But you can still ensure that every member of your team feels they have contributed to building the mission statement — and that will ensure that they all feel ownership of it, and take responsibility to bring it to pass.

This is a key means to organizational alignment.

Step one in preparing a mission statement is to focus on some key words and phrases that describe what is at the heart of what your organization is trying to do. Here, you can easily involve everyone in the organization, through group meetings, using part of normal staff meetings, or asking for written or verbal suggestions.

These brainstorming efforts will give you a very good idea of what your people think is the mission of your company; many will be right, and will provide useful phrases that will be incorporated into your mission statement. Those who are not in tune with your purpose will provide you with information about your need for education, communication, and possible changes, on the road to alignment.

When you are convinced that you have captured the key concepts that sum up the means to the ends of your organization, put it into words. And the words are important here — work hard to be sure the words accurately convey what you are about, without carrying accidental baggage that will get in the way.

And again, be sure that honesty rules — phrases that seem to contain promises that will be not fulfilled will simply lead to unhappy employees or customers who will come to you with the mission statement held high, demanding why you said this when it clearly is not true.

Never forget that these statements we are working through are intended for just that purpose: to allow everyone connected with your organization to read them, understand what the organization wants to be and to do, and then to test and see if it is really true.

The values and beliefs, coupled with the mission statement, clearly define what your organization is all about.

With this in hand, any of your departments can go through the same process to determine if they are aligned — heading in the same direction as the organization of which they are a part.

ORGANIZATIONAL DIRECTION

DEPARTMENTAL DIRECTION

INDIVIDUAL DIRECTION

Every manager, every employee, can do the same thing. And if they know the organization is standing honestly on those values, and following that mission statement, they can quickly test if they are in alignment. If not, they will have a clear guide to show them how to become aligned, or, if they choose not to, it will be clear their future lies outside your organization.

Each employee can determine where their job fits into the departmental and corporate picture.

In fact, you can have three levels of your foundation. Many organizations are now discovering the value of establishing a corporate statement of values and mission; then developing departmental statements of values and mission; and finally assisting employees in the development of individual values and mission statements. It can be a very exciting project, to help employees who have just showed up for work for the past 10 years, to put on paper the reasons they exist, both on the job and on their own time. We believe that time spent in such an exercise can be a valuable process for an organization of any size.

There are a few mistakes that can typically derail the process of developing a mission statement.

One common error is not pointing the mission statement into the future — not looking ahead far enough. For example, at one point, not many years ago, the railroad companies of North America were actually in the best position to be the major player in transportation services in North America. But to do so, they would have had to expand their vision, and thus their mission statement. They saw their mission as running railroads, instead of offering transportation services.

That may sound like an exercise in words, but think about it — it shows the difference between a mission only for today, and a mission that will not only express the organization's current role, but also carry it into the future. The latter is a mission that is driven by an understanding of the present and future needs of the stakeholders. Dr. Stephen Covey talks about "stakeholder streams" and the need to know where they will take you; missing out will leave you high and dry — perhaps on a railroad with nowhere to go.

Another error is to establish a time-limited target. While that may be temporarily inspiring, when the time runs out or the target is reached, you can have a very confused organization. We suspect this is what has plagued NASA since its stated goal of putting a man on the moon was reached. While that was an inspiring goal, it was not a mission statement — it was time-limited and goal-oriented, and its completion left an organization struggling to define itself and justify its existence.

NASA could learn something from the TV and movie hit, Star Trek, which has a marvelous mission statement: *"To explore strange new worlds, to seek out new life and new civilizations, to boldly go where no one has gone before"*.

This clearly identifies the most important things for the voyagers on the Enterprise to focus on. It provides insight on how things need to be carried out. It identifies what the limitations are, if any. It spells out who they are, what they are doing, and how they should go about doing it.

A third error comes back to a theme we have touched on before: an organization that fails to live by their stated mission.

For example, their mission statement will include phrases like: "to provide the best customer service in our industry" and "to ensure employee satisfaction and career growth opportunities." And then, month by month, they measure dollars. And they don't measure or even consider anything else. They don't ask their customers to rate their service; they don't ask their employees for input about job satisfaction. They don't offer training opportunities.

That organization has made two mistakes. It has failed to be honest about a key part of its mission: to make a profit. And it has built in some statements (good ones, in fact, if they lived by them) without really caring about them.

Another mistake is failing to communicate, in an ongoing fashion, the mission to the employees. Your people need to know what this means to them. They need to hear a commitment to the issues where they are the beneficiaries — like training or employee satisfaction. And, as importantly, they need to hear how their job fits into the mission statement.

For example, if customer satisfaction is part of the mission statement, the employees need to see how they are key to accomplishing that mission, and what role they have in this. Their dealings with the customers are the keys to success.

Furthermore, if your organization is serious about this, you probably need to implement a reward or incentive plan so that employees who go over and above their stated duties to bring the mission into being are recognized and rewarded. More about this in the chapter on structure and systems.

You also need to communicate about the mission with your customers. It can be a very valuable tool to let your customers know why you exist, and how high your level of commitment is to some areas that are of vital importance to them as your clients.

The next time you are at a meeting of people from a number of organizations, try a test — see how long it takes to find someone who thinks that mission statements are a joke.

We suspect you will find that person really fast. Why? Because too many organizations have done the politically correct thing, and thrown together a nice-sounding mission statement, which has been ignored ever since. It's better not to do one at all.

But best is to do it right, and then use it right. If a mission statement is properly implemented, it can be extremely effective and powerful in your organization. You can keep it front and centre, review it at weekly meetings, and test new projects and ideas against it. It will help you to decide what is important and what is busy-work — what is carrying you toward accomplishment of your mission statement. It will help you to decide where to put your resources, your people, your dollars.

It not only reminds you where you want to go; it helps you to get there.

Management Principles

"Management principles" is a twenty-dollar phrase for a million-dollar question: How do we want to treat one another?

We have adopted the term "management principles" because it's usually at the management level where these concepts are first examined and implemented. They are considered to be the leaders within the organization.

But the truth is these are principles that must come to apply across the board, throughout the company, top to bottom. If these principles are to be effective, they have to be practiced by everyone.

Maybe it would be better to talk about "people principles".

A good way to gain a perspective on this is to imagine yourself hired as the manager of a new organization. You have to decide how you're going to manage — what are the principles that will guide you?

So you start your list of principles: *You will treat your employees with respect at all times. You will lead by example. You will take responsibility. You will work hard and play hard. You will be financially frugal.*

You want to communicate them to your new employees, because you would like to see them adopt the same principles in their approach to their work, and to their fellow workers.

But you realize there is also a risk to telling them what your management principles are, because you will have given them another set of benchmarks by which to judge you.

These, then, are the operational benefits of developing a set of management principles: you will develop a strong and positive set of principles to live and to work by; you will begin to communicate them and see them come to life within your team; and you will have added the enforcement factor — the fact that your people are watching you will help you to stick to the principles you have developed.

Management principles are internal. They may parallel your organization's values and beliefs in some areas, but they are concerned primarily with how you and your people treat one another.

This is often where the rubber hits the road. A corporate

value may be expressed as "financial success." A management principle arising from that would be "frugality". And this would come to life when managers and employees fly economy class, or share rooms when they have to be on the road. You won't find economy flights in the mission statement or the values and beliefs, but they are in alignment with them, and arise naturally from thoughtful and consistently-practiced management principles.

Management principles are not like speed limits — they do not set absolute limits or boundaries. They will not result in a group of 20 or 20,000 managers acting identically. But they will give those managers an identical base on which to develop individual, but aligned, behaviours.

Developing management principles

How do you go about developing management principles? First, let's realize that your organization already has a long list of unstated management principles. The fact that the list is unstated probably means that it is inconsistent, with some good principles and some questionable concepts that will not stand up well under examination. So, let's examine them.

Start by asking your managers to identify the principles by which they manage, by which they relate to their staff members. What are their cornerstones? People being people, this will probably get you the positives, only. That's okay.

Next, ask them, trying for as much honesty as possible, if the employees reporting to them would recognize their list as being theirs? This is when managers start to realize that some of their stated principles are simply wishes, which are never realized. Getting that out in the open is the first step to making them real; and in doing so, most of the unstated negatives will be revealed as inadequate or undesirable.

Now, bring the managers together to brainstorm and to cull the list of management principles. Remember that you want to develop a set of principles that represent how you want to treat your people; and that this will be a public list, so your people can call you on it if you are ignoring your principles. Keeping these two things in mind will keep you on track toward a meaningful and reasonable set of management principles.

Again, depending on your size and structure, you can do this with managers only, or with all staff. You may also want to allow individual departments to develop their own, unique set of management principles, as long as they are in alignment with the foundational elements of the rest of the organization.

We need to note at this point that, the more individuals you can get involved in the development process in any of these areas, the better. Prior to the production of any "published document", there needs to be development of "draft documents". This should allow all members of the organization to provide feedback and input.

It is critical that there is participation by all members of your organization in the development process. From this point on, please keep this in mind.

One fine organization we know took six months to develop their set of management principles. Then, they printed them, laminated them, and gave one to every employee.

From then on, every time a manager met with an employee, the employee knew the ethical ground rules — how the company wanted people to treat each other. "Respect one another" said the laminated sheet, and that no longer left any room for managers to start screaming at employees. The published list kept managers on track, but it also helped improve management-staff relationships enormously. That one sheet of paper was and is a very valuable management tool.

Obviously, this can be quite difficult for some managers. Because in most organizations, there is a traditional power boundary that keeps all the power in the management offices. Simply giving the employees that piece of paper meant giving away a lot of managerial power.

But organizations which are succeeding have already figured out that in today's world, good managers are managers who give up power. Leadership, today, means facilitating, delegating, nurturing, co-operating. It does not mean brow-beating or behaving in a tyrannical manner. Those days are gone.

We're not talking about managerial wimps, here.

Perhaps the best model is that of a good parent. Parenting is a two-decade long surrendering of power. Obviously, you don't give up all power when the child is 18 months old. You still maintain a lot of authority, for the child's good.

No parent says to a two-year-old, "I'm not telling you whether or not to touch that red-hot burner, because I want you to be responsible and mature in your decision-making."

But a few years later, hot burners are the child's exclusive responsibility; the parent doesn't worry about that issue any more, and the child has more personal authority, more power.

The same must be true in our organizations, today, if we are to develop flexible, able employees ready to meet the new challenges that come to us all, daily.

But it is a gradual process. This is where the popular idea of empowerment may have faltered — not in concept, but in practice. Too many managers have been struck by this new idea, rushed back to the office or plant, and handed too much power over too quickly. There has to be a building of skill, and of confidence, and trust must be in place, both ways.

And to slip in a related thought: let's not pretend that all employees — or managers — will be ideal people fostering an ideal environment. There will still be problems, and there will still be need for discipline. However, clearly articulated management principles provide a much firmer foundation for organizational discipline. They clear up confusion, and remove all of the subjectivity that is probably the largest pitfall in the corporate disciplinary procedure, today.

Management principles also provide a foundation for discipline in the other meaning of the word. They give an operational structure in which your people can understand how they should relate to one another and to their jobs. They provide an underpinning for self-discipline.

Let's get back on the plane for a moment. If your employee has never seen a set of management principles, he or she may be tempted to fly first-class across the continent. But he or she may also feel somewhat guilty for ripping off the company, and may even start to bury some of those expenses to avoid the confrontation that may or may not be coming. The employee is not even sure if he or she is doing something wrong.

Members of your organization need to understand what the parameters of the "Values and Beliefs" and the "Management Principles" mean in their day to day behaviour. These should help to clarify whether flying first class across the continent is part of how your organization operates. When the first entry in his or her daily calendar is a sheet of principles that include being frugal to contribute to corporate financial health, for example, there is a real incentive to self-discipline.

Putting management principles into practice

Once you have your management principles in writing, take time to think about and to discuss how they can be put into practice. This will change from department to department and from situation to situation, but it is good to see how a principle becomes a practice.

For example, there may be a management principle that says, "We will provide growth opportunities for our employees." Great. How are you going to do that? A suggestion would be to take each management principle and identify daily practices/behaviours that support this principle.

One manager may initiate brown-bag seminars at lunch. Another may meet one on one with his or her people to develop individual personal development action plans.

Some may make sure that part of every staff meeting is devoted to personal development, in one way or another.

In another case, the principle may be frugality. Your organization may want to reward employees who save the company money.

So, the management principle is clear, but you must then proceed one step further to put it into practice, appropriately, in your environment. Any foundational step that does not lead to action is a step wasted.

Key Result Areas

Key Result Areas (KRAs) are the indicators of success and balance within the organization. We place a very high emphasis on KRAs, because properly developed and monitored KRAs will give you a full-spectrum picture of the success of your organization, unlike any you have had before.

Many companies judge their success based solely on bottom line. Now, while bottom line is vitally important — it can mean life or death for your organization — it is not the only important thing. There are other areas, too, that relate just as significantly to corporate health.

A company with bottom-line tunnel vision is like a doctor who always checks your heart, but ignores brain, lungs and limbs. KRAs are the answer.

We develop KRAs by looking at all the foundation stones already discussed. Ask yourself, based on your stakeholder needs, your values, and your mission — What are the most important indicators of your organization's success?

And how can you measure them to track if you are heading in a "success direction"?

To do this right requires some paradigm shifting. We need to think clearly about what we know to be true success indicators. For example: in our personal life, what have we been told success is all about? In many instances we have been programmed to consider the external elements of success, such as our career growth, our financial position, or the 'toys' that we acquire. But maybe — in fact, undoubtedly — there are other factors. Maybe success also means having a happy family life, or being involved in your community, or good health, or strong relationships with friends.

In other words, there are many areas of balance that do not have to take away from career and financial success, but need to be considered when you, personally, are building a successful life.

The same is true of a company. A profitable company with very unhappy employees, for example, may be seen as a success because of the monthly financial report, but is not really succeeding. And it is very likely it will not even succeed financially, a few years or maybe even just a few months down the road.

We've all heard of companies that sacrifice research and development or technological upgrading in order to drop more dollars to the bottom line. Then they are sold, and the new buyer discovers the profits were temporary, and the problems, terminal. No one was assessing all of the Key Result Areas before that change of ownership.

So start your discussion of KRAs with this question:

based on our values, mission and stakeholder needs, what does success mean to us?

Don't take any easy answers, like "15% return on revenue" — get behind that by asking, what factors are important to ensure we can produce that kind of profit, or even improve on it? Your answers to that one question may be "happy customers", "motivated sales staff" or "improved products". Now you have started to identify some Key Result Areas.

KRAs are where the rubber hits the road. This is your mechanism to assess your organization on a regular basis. KRAs give you a well-balanced, holistic top and bottom line that includes dollars, but goes well beyond that one-dimensional, traditional measurement of corporate success.

Organizations that measure only dollars are really focusing on one stakeholder group — the owners. There may be some consideration of the employees (profit may mean job security) but the needs of customers are completely ignored. This is a recipe for short-term corporate life.

You need to be able to identify and track Key Result Areas that relate to all stakeholders, and to all the needs of the stakeholders; to your values, and your mission, and your vision for the future.

So you want to discover, what are your success indicators?

(One thought to consider here is where financial success enters into the "foundation areas". Many organizations do not include financial success in their "value statements", but do consider it a reward for the services they render. In this way, they see areas such as "profit" not as a value, but most definitely as a Key Result Area. There is no right or wrong answer to this, but this issue needs to be discussed and understood as to where this fits within your organizational culture.)

Back to success indicators: once you know what they are, how do you *measure* them? The easiest to measure are those that can be counted: dollars, number of sales, employee retention levels. But don't limit yourself. If you can't be entirely objective, be subjective.

For example, we want happy employees. We want there to be a fun atmosphere in our department. So how many days this week was it fun? Five of six? — that's pretty good. Friday afternoon only? Not so good. You don't need a number on everything to be able to assess every Key Result Area that you have identified as important.

KRAs can be developed for your organization, for individual departments, and for each person in your organization. They will not be identical, but they must be aligned.

You can learn something from this. If your employees believe growth opportunities are an important measure of success in their jobs, and your organization says nothing about that, you're out of alignment. On the other hand, if your organization prizes independent thinking and intrapreneurship, and you have employees for whom showing up is their top objective, you're also out of alignment.

However, if your organization keys on sales growth as a KRA, and one department has "staff development", is that out of alignment? Probably not — development will produce better sales people, if the training is in alignment with organizational objectives.

Even here there is need for constant communication and KRA awareness — when dealing with training, for example, be sure the training supplied is really in alignment with your organizational objectives. We know of one company where the sales staff was asking for computer training, which on the surface seems a valid request. But they wanted the training, not to do their job better, but because the highly-computerized creative department was in the next office, and the sales reps thought the computers were neat.

You will need to drive KRA thinking through every area in your organization. Because if every employee knows what makes a successful day for him or her, based on alignment with your mission, you're in pretty good shape.

But it doesn't work if your managers decide that one KRA is excellence in customer service, but you have not communicated that to your staff. A receptionist who thinks a good day is making it to work on time will not be contributing to success in a key area.

One warning: developing KRAs will cause paradigm shifting all along the line. For example, a sales rep who has been conditioned to believe success means high commissions at the cost of everything else may come to realize that success also means providing excellent service to his or her customers, even if a "service call" doesn't lead to an immediate commission cheque. The rep must shift paradigms, to adopt a different view of success in selling. He or she must come to realize that service-oriented sales will, in fact, produce a solid, long-term relationship with the customer, and this will mean business for the organization, and regular paycheques over the long haul.

Allowing your people to find broad-based, holistic success will mean much higher employee retention, fewer sick days, and fewer stress-related crisis in general.

Your organization will be tracking success on the long term.

CHAPTER FOUR: KEY NOTE REVIEW

• Values and beliefs represent the cornerstone of your organization. By cornerstone, we mean that they should truly identify what you are all about and how you are going to operate.

The values and beliefs should be used for all-important decision making and provide the 'guiding light' in delicate matters that need to be addressed.

- **Organizational Mission Statements (examples):**

FUSION Consulting Inc.

We are dedicated to assisting individuals in diverse organizations, in the development of the human energy, growth, and commitment of each team member. In this way, we seek to make the world a better place to live.

OTIP/RAEO — Ontario Teachers Insurance Plan

OTIP/RAEO is committed to providing quality insurance benefits for the best value. We will accomplish this through product and service excellence to meet the unique needs of Ontario's educational employees.

Niagara Falls Hydro Electric Commission:

The Niagara Falls Hydro Electric Commission is committed to our Customers, to supply electricity in a safe, efficient, economical and reliable manner.

Working together to manage our resources today and for the future.

Ontario Clean Water Agency

To be the best in the business of producing clean water and promoting its wise use.

McKenzie Medical Center/ West Tennessee Women's Center

It shall be the mission of the McKenzie Medical Center/West Tennessee Women's Center to provide quality and compassionate care to all of our patients with regard to them as individuals, as family members, and as members of our community and greater society. Further, we shall endeavor to be personally and professionally respectful and supportive of one another as health care providers in recognition of the necessity of support as an essential factor in pursuit of our stated goal.

VERSA Services Ltd.

We are committed to lead in the management and provision of high quality food, beverage, cleaning and other services, to exceed the expectations of the people we serve.

Maritime Life — Ontario Client Service Centre

The Mission of the Ontario Client Service Centre is to provide our customers the highest quality, personalized service in Group Benefits. The growth of our business is a direct result of the unique abilities of our people.

Boonstra Heating & Air Conditioning

We dedicate ourselves to exceeding our customers' expectations in providing the highest standard of satisfaction.

We believe in partnerships with customers and employees which are built on our values and beliefs.

We enjoy stability and growth by achieving excellence through our skilled, professional people.

We secure our reputation as the best in the industry

through our commitment to this mission.

Colour Technologies Limited

Colour Technologies will provide superior graphic communications services by combining craftsmanship, state of the art technology and a dedication to excellence.

Stentor International Mission (Draft version)

Through people, alliances and teamwork develop world class global telecommunications solutions, to enable the Stentor Alliance to be a leading provider of international services.

The principal focus of Stentor International is to profitably protect and grow the international revenues of the Stentor owner companies by meeting the needs of their customers.

T. J Watson Enterprises O/A Tim Horton Donuts

Our Mission

We are committed to establishing service and quality as a lifestyle, through the development of individual growth and teamwork.

• **Mission Statements:**

Mission statements define why your organization exists. Key questions to consider in reviewing your organization's mission:

- Does it relate to all Stakeholders? Do they see what's in it for them?
- Does it describe the best possible organization?
- Can the mission statement assist in solving conflicts between priorities?
- Does the mission statement assist us in:
    * making day-to-day decisions?
    * feeling secure and worthwhile?
    * identifying how we influence others?
- Does our mission statement provide direction, challenge and motivation both today and for the future?
- Does our mission statement identify both the 'doing good' and economic needs of our organization?

- To build a mission statement, get those directly involved in the particular area of your organization and brainstorm with them in developing, from the heart and the head, the purpose of your organization.

• **Management Principles:**

Management Principles represent **'how we want to treat one another'** within the organization. **They are there whether you put them in writing or not!**

• **Key Result Areas:**

Key Result Areas are built on the foundations of values and beliefs, mission and managing principles, along with a clear understanding of the needs and wants of your Stakeholders - which identify why your organization exists.

Strive for alignment and balance in their development and work on how you are going to measure them, from both an organizational and an individual perspective.

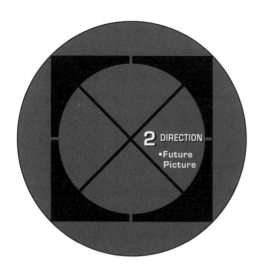

CHAPTER FIVE
FUTURE PICTURE

Wilfrid Laurier University in Waterloo, Ontario has been growing, modestly, over the past few decades. The university's leaders realized that they had been addressing the physical growth in a piece-meal fashion, with no organized plan of what the institution would look like in the future, given the past growth trends. There had not been enough serious consideration given to the big picture. This particular school is quite hemmed in by the city around it, and they began to realize this could become a problem.

So the school initiated the project, Vision 2020. They brought in architectural and design experts to look at the land they owned, past growth trends, the present situation, successes and failures.

Then the design groups projected what the campus might look like in the year 2020. They discovered some interesting growth and development patterns that had never been specifically identified. They also projected school population based on past trends. In addition, they considered the present architecture on the campus, and designed future buildings with this in mind.

In the designs that came back they considered enough about the university to identify potential problems, such as parking. They were also able to move backward from the future picture to today, to build and begin to implement a blue print of how to get to Vision 2020, in order to be ready for 2020.

This is the value of visioning, of spending time to develop a future picture.

It rests on your understanding of your stakeholder needs, and on the foundation we have already built in the preceding chapters. Architects who did not understand that students and staff — all stakeholders — need places for their cars, as well as for themselves, would not have been able to project a future picture.

Your future picture looks at your organizational potential three, five, ten or twenty years down the road.

Here's a good definition:

Your vision will be your framework which guides those choices which determine the nature and direction of your organization.

"Framework" means this is a guide, a structure within which flexibility and growth are possible. For example, a person may have this vision: "I want to save enough money to be able to retire at 50." That's the framework. It allows flexibility of investment strategy, but is a reminder that a two-month vacation next year may not fit into the larger framework.

Future picture is *not* a long-range plan, as this has traditionally been understood. Today, to do a long-range plan makes no sense. Long-range plans, typical in the 70s and 80s, were basically financial plans, projected and laid out in detail over several years. This no longer works.

With change as constant and as rapid as it is today, long range plans simply limit flexibility. It is just no longer reasonable to try to work on the details, five years hence. Too much will change.

To go back to our friend who wants to retire at 50, deciding now to invest $10,000 a year in RSPs over the next 15 years would be a typical long-range plan. But it leaves no flexibility for changing tax laws, windfall income, or investment opportunities.

In our world, inflexible long-range planning will not work; setting a vision, though, is crucial.

Instead, we craft a future picture, which sets a broad target, and then we allow flexibility and change in the way we move toward that future. This flexibility is very, very important.

Setting your future picture starts with blue-sky visioning.

Brainstorm. Talk about your stakeholders and their needs; imagine your potential.

We suggest thinking of this as a funnel process. In other words, at the beginning, there is room for anything. As you talk and think and process, many of those initial ideas will be discarded as the funnel narrows, and you begin to fine-tune your focus. But there's lots of room at the beginning, at the top of the funnel.

Start by looking back. From a historical perspective, where have you come from? What have been your successes, and your failures? What skills and competencies now exist in your organization? What have you traditionally been good at? What changes have you see in the past five or ten years? This will be useful when you begin to picture the changes likely to come in the future.

Then, decide on the parameters of your visioning. Are you looking at your physical plant, or at potential products, at financial areas, at human resources? Most often, you will want to deal with all of these areas, but don't skip this step — it helps you identify them, instead of becoming locked into one stream, only. You'll also want to set your time frame — is your vision focused on five, ten or 20 years down the road?

Now, start brainstorming. Start the visioning.

You should realize that doing this right takes longer than you think. This won't be easy, because visioning will never appear to be urgent. It's important, but it doesn't feel like it's urgent. The value from this process will come from 'painting a potential picture' of where your organization is going, and thinking about the important considerations in developing this vision.

The urgency will become apparent only when it is too late to set direction, when those five years are behind you, and so is the opportunity for ongoing success.

This process can be extremely dynamic, especially if it is given the time and attention that it deserves. And it does deserve it — you're setting the direction for your company over the next decade or two! So spend the time. Look at all the "blue sky" ideas, kick them around, evaluate them. Be creative and bold.

Then you will start to consolidate, to refine.

Don't worry about absolute accuracy — you are being a visionary, not a prophet. You won't be stoned at the gates if you are not completely dead-on right.

But if you take the time, your organization will be much more right when you reach the future than it would have been had you not made this investment of time and energy in your future.

Many companies discover that this can be a frightening process. Why? Because they find themselves in a Catch-22 situation. They look to the future *and they're not in it*.

For example, many organizations which are currently quite financially successful may realize, through this process, that their products will not be necessary, ten years from now. But they're doing fine today.

Now what? Do they divert some of those profits into research and development to guarantee long-term viability, or do they keep making the profit and try and stretch it as long as they can? It can be a tough choice — but with a future picture in front of them, it will be an informed choice.

And setting the future picture will give them a fighting chance to make the changes that will mean they will exist and thrive five or ten years from now. If you don't do it, your future may be very brief, indeed.

Setting your vision should also provide a direction for research and development in your organization. We have developed a format entitled "Richly Imagined Future".

Here are two sets of sample questions, the first which can be used to prepare managers to begin the visioning process; the second, to help you develop your Richly Imagined Future:

Visioning Process Pre-Meeting Questions:

In preparation for our session, please consider the following questions as they apply to our organization. Please document your thoughts on this paper, and bring them to the session.

Where have we come from? (Consider the past 5 years)

Where are we now?

What are the noted changes between past and present?

What changes do we see in the future?

External influences affecting us:

Internal, in our organization:

What needs to be altered internally, within our organization?

(Please also complete the following:)

Richly Imagined Future:

In looking ahead to the future, consider the following areas in developing the picture for our organization.

1) What and who will be our major competition?

2) How will we be able to use technology to leverage our business?

3) What will (or may be) some of the shifts in the ways and means that we are presently doing business (what needs to shift?).

4) What changes to do we see from a Human Resources perspective?

5) Consider the physical space requirements; what changes do we foresee?

6) What changes do we see with our customer base?

7) What are the Growth areas for us to focus on (what are the new KRAs)?

8) Are there any market opportunities that we should consider?

9) Are there any political or geographic considerations?

10) What changes do we see from a product or service change perspective?

11) What are our specific strategic intents (desires or goals)?

VISIONING PROCESS FUNNEL

HISTORICAL PERSPECTIVE

VISION CRITERIA

**IDEAS:
ANALYSIS &
LOOKING TO
THE FUTURE**

Consolidate into
a unified picture
for the future

VISION
(Potential Future Picture)

At the end of the funnel, what you want to walk away with through all this analysis is the *potential future picture* — the vision toward which you want to work.

So now, you have built the foundation for your organization, and you have identified the framework within which you can build. And all of this is in alignment.

Now you can begin to look at what you need to do, now: Today's Issues.

CHAPTER FIVE: KEY NOTE REVIEW

• The visioning process should include dealing with the important realities and priorities of today and the future. Reflecting on the past provides valuable insight to build the future picture.

• Remember that this represents a 'possible future', which means that it could change. As in the other foundation areas, you need to review the vision on a regular basis, and keep it up to date.

• Take the time to analyze the potential, by answering the questions that will identify the ingredients of your future picture.

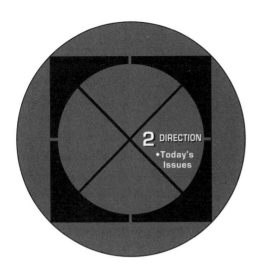

CHAPTER SIX
TODAY'S ISSUES

Now, let's look at the issues you are facing today. What does your organization need to deal with on the shorter term? Let's develop a tactical plan for the next 12 to 18 months.

Many organizations approach this using what they call a **SWOT** analysis: looking at **S**trengths, **W**eakness, **O**pportunities, and **T**hreats.

This may be a little less complicated than building your future picture, but the methodology is very much the same. We start by reviewing the stakeholder needs, our values, mission, management principles and future vision, and from this we identify issues that our organization needs to address in the next 12 to 24 months.

Clarity is important. Once you have brainstormed, consolidate and define. Pull related issues together. Be sure everyone within your organization understands what these issues are.

And then, after everyone clearly understands what these issues are, prioritize them. You'll need to decide which issues really need your attention over the next 12 months. And be practical — you know, full well, that you cannot continue to operate effectively while trying to address 53 newly identified issues!

The CEO of a hospital we have worked with has said "We will take on no more than three issues in the next 12 months, but we want to have those done with, addressed, and handled." We have also seen companies who could not pare down their list to less than 20 — but who had addressed only one, a year later. The former approach, although it may appear rigid or limiting, is obviously better than the latter.

We suggest working with three to seven "today's issues". The end result of this process is to develop goals and strategies for those three to seven issues.

A **goal** has a clearly defined end. (For example: We will reduce employee turn-over to 5% by the end of next year.) In developing goals, the following outline may be of assistance in their creation:

S - Simple - one written page in easy-to-understand language.
M - Manageable - no more than 3 to 8 in number.
A - Attainable - goals are not unattainable dreams, but stretch areas.
R - Relevant - they are based on what is important.
T - Time Bound - there is an end point, by which the goal must be reached.

A **strategy** is a position taken. A strategy can work toward a goal. (For example: We will develop programs aimed toward having happier employees.) In developing strategies, you can utilize the SMART format, except there may not be a defined end, as there is with goals.

Here are some other examples of goals and strategies.

Goals might include:

• Hit our defined financial targets.

• Work with x number of firms in the next 12 months.

• Develop x number of marketing initiatives before the end of this year.

• Sign x number of planning contracts this year.

Strategies might include:

• Quality service approach to all clients.

• Continue technological development and investment

• Begin a transition to a principle-based training organization.

Strategies, as we have mentioned, do not have a defined

end. They are a tack you are taking, usually as part of a plan to reach one of your goals or, on the larger, longer picture, to take your organization toward the future picture you have already developed.

Please understand that we are not calling on you or your organization to suddenly develop an unerring ability to foretell the future. Your first set of goals and strategies should almost be seen as a draft; you can come back to it, revise it. A list of today's issues is a tool for you to use; it is not a tyrant which will direct your organization, no matter what.

In simple terms, your goals and strategies for today's issues are your best guess about the things you need to work on, right now and through the next twelve months. They can change in ways that your foundation blocks will not.

For example, if your organization is an insurance brokerage, one group of stakeholders will be your clients, and your foundation blocks will relate to being the best insurance brokerage possible. These things don't change.

But let's say your company has set a goal of increasing sales by 10% this year, you've put appropriate strategies in place, but then the government passes new legislation that takes over one-third of your normal business, and one of your managing partners takes a sudden early retirement and moves to Tahiti. You will want to revisit and probably change many of your goals and strategies. But your foundation will remain intact.

The first stage, as we have noted, is to establish your top three to seven goals for the year. Take into account your strengths and weaknesses — both will be important in helping you to deal with today's issues.

Your strengths will give you resources to tackle those issues. Your weaknesses will probably become those issues, and you will want to set goals and strategies related to solving them. Of course, you will also want to set goals and strategies related to new opportunities; today's issues will probably be a combination of weaknesses needing a solution, opportunities, and responses to threats.

Part of the process will be checking your Key Result Areas. Remember, you want to review these on a regular basis, anyway, and during this process you are more likely to identify weaknesses, and even opportunities.

Now, once you have your list of three to seven goals for the next 12 months, you need to decide how you are going to address them. You need to decide on a plan or road map, to put some structure around the goals (destination).

Goals and strategies need to be very specific, in two ways. They need to be well defined, and they need to be well understood. Scope them out. Understand your present situation, the resources needed to accomplish the goal, the implications for your organization if the goal is reached. At the end of this chapter, we will outline a process for you to work with to accomplish this end.

One particular organization set a goal of increasing sales. One of their strategies was to bring on board some top-notch salespeople. This was a good strategy.

Another strategy should have been to plan for increased production. But they didn't consider that element, and found themselves with product sold that was not produced, and was unlikely to be produced any time in the near future. Their goal was scuttled by incomplete planning.

Another small business — a butcher shop — had the idea of holding an open house, with a barbecue, and inviting customers to sample their wares. They had not advertised much before, but they bought full-page ads in their local paper to announce this event.

It was a spectacular success — measured on customer interest. But the owners of the shop had failed to staff adequately for such a day, and by the end of the experience, employers and employees alike decided they never wanted to go through that again. Unfortunately, they solved that problem by discontinuing the program, cancelling all advertising, and reverting to being the small, sleepy business they were at the start, sort of an early retirement among the meat trays.

So it is important to understand your goals and strategies — both what they mean (by definition), and also what they could mean to your organization (if they are accomplished).

Once you are relatively confident that you understand your goals, you will want to formulate some action steps, assign responsibility, and set some deadlines. All too often, a goal is set, with a final deadline, and when that time comes, the same people sit at a table and wonder why nothing was accomplished.

Set interim deadlines for smaller tasks; clearly assign responsibility; follow up.

Take the goal apart. Divide it into chunks. This can happen in at least two ways — if the goal applies to the whole organization, decide what chunks each department is responsible for. And in the individual departments, split it up as suggested above: divide your 12-month goal into weekly chunks. What do we have to accomplish this week to be on track, a year from now? The answer to that is your action plan for this week. Your success at achieving it — as assessed seven days from now — will tell you if you are on track to meet that goal or not.

You won't succeed, every week. But you have a far better chance of accomplishing your 12-month goal if you can correct a small failure on a weekly basis, instead of waiting 12 months to discover you never got out of the starting blocks.

And be sure that every employee understands his or her responsibility, his or her role in reaching this goal. An employee who understands where he or she fits in is an employee likely to be in alignment with the organization, and more than likely to be a happy employee.

Here's an example of how this might work with one of today's issues: employee morale.

As a manager, you meet with the entire staff, and ask the question: How can we improve employee morale? You make sure the staff understands this is a brainstorming session; all ideas are welcome, but not all ideas will be adopted. This is a time to get everything on the table; later, you will sift and sort.

When lots of ideas have come forward, you start the sifting process. Some won't work — your organization doesn't have the resources to send all employees to Hawaii for R and R. Some are related, and can be categorized together, like suggestions about ball tournaments, parties, and so on that might be listed as "recreational opportunities".

One problem identified through this brainstorming session is that the employees feel a lack of communication with management. That one sits squarely on your shoulders. So you develop a number of strategies. One is to spend individual time with each employee.

This is where the idea must be put into practice. You could write that down, promise it to the employees, and check back to see how you're doing, six months from now. That would, most likely, lead to another employee morale problem: managers who don't keep their promises.

A better answer for you, as manager, is to decide how often you should have individual contact with your team. If you decide it should happen every week, then you build that into your planned week, just as you would a scheduled meeting with your supervisor. And you check, every week, to make sure you have kept that commitment — to yourself and to your team.

By using this kind of approach with all of the goals and strategies, you can reduce your employee morale problem into manageable chunks that can be accomplished, and that can be measured on an immediate basis.

The employees know that you plan to meet with each of them, each week. Let's say you miss three of them, one week. If you were waiting for six months to check back, you would have some pretty unhappy staff members. But dealing with goals and strategies in manageable chunks reduces the impact of failure — by Friday, you know you have slipped up. You can either spend time with them that day, or go to them, explain or apologize, and make a commitment to meet with them the next week.

We recommend that people develop what we call their "Perfect Week". Take time to sit down and write out what your ideal week would be, at work and, we suggest, at home and in recreation, as well. If everything went right, how would your week take shape?

Here's one example of a Perfect Week:

* Spend individual time with spouse and each child.

* Play four games of squash.

* Read for at least an hour each day.

* Write a note to a family member or personal friend.

* Think "win/win" in all important relationships.

* Work around the house in a non-business activity.

* Spend an hour each week learning something new about technology.

* Speak to four quality prospects.

* Individual review sessions with each key staff member.

* Project and goal planning.

* Prepare and submit required reports on schedule.

At work (and maybe at home as well, because the principles we are stating work on the home front, too), you will want to include behaviours related to your personal goals and strategies. If you are the manager noted above, your perfect week will include: Meet with each employee.

Arising from the employee morale goals and strategies, it might also include: give opportunity at staff meetings for social conversation. It might include: never raise my voice and always treat individuals with respect.

At the end of the week — which we all know will seldom be perfect — this "Perfect Week" document will give you a standard from which you can judge how you did this week. It will help you move toward behaviours that are in alignment with the direction you, your people and your organization want to go.

These personal chunks will give you concrete actions you can take. They may be very simple, but they can make a profound difference as you attack the wide variety of problems, opportunities and threats that will be part of your daily organizational life.

Here's one more example of a simple behavioural change that could make a great deal of difference in team morale in your organization:

How many times have you been in a one-on-one meeting with your supervisor, and the phone rings? Your boss answers it, and talks for several minutes, while you do nothing. How do you feel? Have you ever done that to someone you supervise? How did they feel?

You might try this helpful behavioural modification: if this is a problem, and you have been preempting personal conversation for the telephone, tell your staff you won't do that any more. Keep that promise. If there ever could be an exception (you're expecting the Prince of Wales to call), warn them this could happen, and give them permission in advance to take a break, or return to their desk until the call is over.

We're sure that when you have been the victim of this behaviour, it has irritated you. Multiply that irritation by the number of employees who have stared out the window while they waited for their meeting to resume and you'll realize you may have found one small step you can take toward happier employees.

Back to the bigger picture: one key to accomplishing goals is to make it easy and understandable for everyone — managers and team members — to act. Everyone needs to know what they must do, on a daily basis, to reach these goals. Otherwise, this just won't work.

A nice corporate blueprint that sits waiting for review at the end of the year will never become reality; weekly action plans, clearly defined, individually assigned and reviewed regularly, will take concrete form, and probably on schedule.

As you work on your personal action plan, week by week, you'll probably find that it will also work on you. By this, we mean that some of your strategies will involve developing new behaviours that will serve you well for the rest of your interactive days! But there is a downside to this, at least initially. The kind of paradigm shifts we are discussing throughout this book — organizationally, departmentally and individually — mean personal change; sometimes, lots of change. And change is never an easy thing to take.

Much has been written — and much of it very good — about the impact of change. We don't intend to reproduce those excellent works. However, we should point out that change can engender a wide variety of emotional and physical responses.

The most dramatic kind of changes usually produce the most dramatic effects; death of a loved one or marital breakdown are typically cited as the changes that cause the greatest impact.

But other changes can have the same effects, usually to a lesser extent, but sometimes with as much impact.

People going through change experience such things as anger, confusion, relief, anxiety, fear, physical illness, joy, loneliness, denial, acceptance, and an entire menu of often contradictory reactions. These are — and this is important to note — normal. In fact, someone reacting normally to a situation of significant change can appear to be seriously emotionally unbalanced. They aren't — change can do that to a person.

Someone who is angry or even sick because his job description has just changed, or because she is now reporting to a co-worker who was once an equal colleague, is not necessarily mean-spirited or small-minded; he or she is just normal. The reality is that people go through a traumatic change process any time they undergo shifts away from customary behavioural habits.

People need time, and sometimes assistance, to work through the change process, which is exactly the same as the grieving process, because every change involves a loss of some kind. Even a promotion means the person is losing the camaraderie with colleagues; a corporate restructuring can mean all kinds of real or perceived losses.

Give people the time and the room, as much as possible, to find their way through the impact of change.

To sum up:

1) On a daily basis, you should be asking, "Are we living up to our values, and are we keeping in touch with our stakeholders?"

2) On a weekly basis, you and all of your team members should be checking on the progress of your chunks of the goals and strategies.

3) As a management team, you now have a framework in which to meet, discuss, and build. As you meet on a regular basis — we suggest monthly meetings — use your Key Result Areas and your goals and strategies as that framework.

Many people will be astonished that we have come this far in the book, and that this will be the first time we will use the following term: "business plan". We believe that only now has the time come to look at developing a business plan. It makes no sense to try to develop a business plan before you thoroughly understand your organization, and set the course for alignment. You might set out a plan, but there would be no chance of bringing it to pass, without this foundational, fundamental work, first of all.

But we acknowledge that business plans are seen as being very important, especially by financial institutions that may very well hold your organization's purse strings. So, now that our foundation is laid and we're taking care of the immediate needs over the next 12 to 24 months, we'll look at developing a business plan. In fact, many elements of your business plan have already been developed.

It's important to keep the bankers happy. However, what we will suggest goes well beyond the financial statement and projection that too many banks and businesses mistake for a valid business plan.

CHAPTER SEVEN: KEY NOTE REVIEW

- **Goals and Strategies Development Process:**

- Based on what has been developed to date, identify what are the 'issues' that need to be in place to reach your future vision, to support your foundation blocks and to address your Stakeholder needs. You may wish to build on this process by identifying your 'Strengths', 'Weaknesses', 'Opportunities' , and 'Threats'.

- After a thoughtful analysis, identify the top three to seven items that need to be addressed in the next 12 months and develop either into goals (specific end results) or strategies (positions to be taken).

- Develop Blue Prints for each goal or strategy, which identify the steps needed to complete the target. This should include; specific action steps; time frames; who is responsible; resources needed; guidelines given.

- Develop an **action plan** for each item (Goal and Strategy) that includes:

- Clear definition of the specific outcome (Why is this important?).

- Scope/size -- the nature of the issue (How big a task is it? What all is involved? What needs to be kept in front of you?).

- Definition of the present situation.

- Identification of the problems/opportunities.

• Brainstorming on "action plan steps" and ideas to address the issue (Develop a coordinated, step-by-step plan to make the goal a reality. For each step identify who is responsible, and all timing deadlines).

• Evaluation after the "action plan steps" are completed to see if the task is "do-able".

• Establishment of a follow-up process to check on your progress.

- Organization Goals and Strategies need to be communicated with all team members. Then, team members need to be engaged — committed to the goals and strategies. In fact, there needs to be a clear indication of what the individual responsibilities or contributions are towards each goal or task.

• **Perfect Week:**

- The 'Perfect Week' identifies the tasks or activities required, if completed, that will ensure meeting the roles/responsibilities and goals for each member of the team. All important aspects of the individual's life need to be included in this process. The weekly planning process should include incorporating these activities.

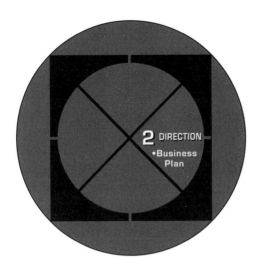

CHAPTER SEVEN
BUSINESS PLAN

Let's make this perfectly clear: what we are talking about here is not a financial statement. We're always astounded when banks are prepared to finance — or refuse to finance — a business, on the basis of a two or three page financial statement. That is not a business plan; it is a description of real or imagined financial success that ignores most of the Key Result Areas that would contribute to — or diminish the chances of — attaining that success.

Such a partial plan is actually of little use to the bank — whatever the loans officer says — and of no use to you in your planning and development process. But we have yet to see any book in regular corporate circulation that tells you how to put a complete, all-encompassing business plan together.

We are talking about developing a business plan which takes everything we've looked at up to now, in chapters one through six, and consolidates it into a clear road map, a plan with carefully defined headings, for the next year to two years.

This obviously presents you — especially as a leader in your organization — with an opportunity to bring together everything you have been looking at, into one consolidated whole.

This differs from Today's Issues in one important way: when you're dealing with Today's Issues, you are acting like a firefighter, looking for the crisis areas and rallying your team to solve them. It is very possible that your five to eight issues included nothing about finances, or about human resources, or about technology, because you realized those particular areas were not potential flash points.

Your business plan must touch all of these, and more. It needs to be an encyclopedic overview of your organization, and where you are going in the near future.

In this way, your business plan differs from your Vision, which carries your company further into the future. The business plan is detailed, and immediate. This may be more than the bank has asked for, but it is the way to make this document of optimum use to you and your organization.

If we ran a bank, we would want to know a lot more

about your organization than a financial statement and projection. We would want to know where you are at with technology. We would ask who your key people are, and if they are likely to remain a resource (continuing with the organization) or turn into competition (leaving to set up on their own). Who are the up-and-comers in your company? We would like to know if your plant is adequate or soon to be outdated.

And frankly, banks aside, we think that you would like to know those things, and other information like this, too. That's how a fully developed business plan is of enormous value to you.

You are going to paint a big picture of your organization, considering all of the following areas:

Plants and processes

Finances

Products and services

Marketing

Technology

Human resources

Leadership — the area with which we are primarily concerned throughout this book.

In developing your business plan, we suggest — as we have with all other areas in the book — that you involve a fair amount of discussion with your people. However, the actual formulation of the plan will probably be a more individual effort, performed by the leader or someone designated by the leader.

As you look at each of the areas noted above, you'll want to ask:

Where are we today?

What improvements are necessary in this area?

How do we accomplish these improvements, area by area?

Is our structure appropriate to our vision?

As we mentioned, we encourage you to talk to your team before actually writing the plan, although the leader will probably write the final draft. You'll find that doing this comprehensive picture will force you to take a position in areas that may not have surfaced earlier in the planning process. You may have avoided consideration of some areas because others have been so pressing. This helps you to step back and look at the entire organization, and where it is going.

You will also be painting a picture that is useful as a tool for review — monthly, six months or a year later, you will want to revisit the plan to see if you are on target. You may find that you are bang on, or that you are off line in some areas, or that the plan was wrong in its projections. Any of those findings is beneficial, as long as you move to correct the problems revealed by the review — fix your weak areas, or edit the business plan.

We believe that a complete business plan will be of value to your organization in a number of ways. We have appeared to be somewhat critical of banks earlier in this chapter, but we actually believe that the days of approved credit based on magic numbers on a spreadsheet are rapidly disappearing. It will not be good enough to produce financial projections — investors are going to demand a complete picture of your organization. Who can blame them?

If you are ready with that picture — realistic, honest, and with challenges anticipated and prospective solutions already in place — your investment credibility will soar.

But while you may or may not present your plan to investors or a bank, you will definitely present it to your team members. This is a very useful tool to let your people in on the big picture of your company. Once the plan is on paper, spend half a day with your people, presenting and discussing your business plan. This is another step to help your organization achieve alignment.

Empowerment

This is probably a good time to raise a very important point, with which we will close this chapter. It concerns the popular concept of empowerment.

It often seems that every second consultant and every second book for managers deals with empowerment — giving power to your employees. This is the way of the future, they say.

We suggest it is only one third of the way of the future. In an effective company, there are actually three interacting principles: empowerment, individual responsibility, and alignment. You can't, as they say, have one without the other.

Everyone is enamoured with the idea of empowerment, not only because it is one of the newest things, but because it really is a very good idea. It is important to allow your employees to make decisions, to be in charge as far as possible of the work they do.

But this only works if those employees show individual responsibility. Too often an outside expert will suggest to an organization that it needs to empower its employees, and the employees receive this as notification of a new employees' right. In reality, it is notification of the need for individual responsibility — because an employee should not be empowered if her or she is not a responsible team member. And, we suggest, some of the empowerment systems ignore this key principle, and that is a road to disaster. Empowering someone who actually believes they have fulfilled their job requirements by showing up is a useless and, in fact, destructive exercise.

How do you judge how much power to give to your employees? On the twin bases of individual responsibility and alignment. If the employee is responsible — engaged, dependable, competent — and aligned — eager to work for the good of the organization — then he or she can be trusted with considerable power and authority, and should be supported and encouraged by their managers at every turn.

If not, the issue becomes simple: get into alignment, or get a new job. This, too, is part of empowerment.

CHAPTER SEVEN: KEY NOTE REVIEW

• The **Business Plan** represents the encyclopedic overview of your organization's key operational areas and the 'plan' therein.

• Business Plan areas addressed (some of the key questions to consider):

Today's Environment
* From an overview perspective, how would we describe the environment?
* What has changed, is changing or in the process of changing in our environment?

Competition
* Who are they?
* What are their strengths and weaknesses?
* What can we learn from the competition?

Products and services
* Do they meet the Customers' needs?
* Are they the right products and services?

Marketing
* Are our marketing efforts effective?
* What have been our strengths in marketing?

Physical plant
* Are the present facilities adequate?
* What are our needs, from a facilities perspective?

Processes of operation
* Are our present processes the most efficient and

effective means of operation?

* Where are the 'roadblocks' in our present processes?

Technology
  * Do we have the right technology to truly leverage all areas of our business?
  * Are we utilizing the technology we have?
  * What are the possibilities with our existing technology?

Human Resources
  * Are our existing human resources adequate?
  * What needs exist regarding development of our human resources?
  * Do we need to consider any changes in our human resources?

Other 'systems' or 'structures' not covered
  * Are our systems supportive and aligned with our direction?
  * What systems or structures are mis-aligned?

* **Tie all the above to the needs of Stakeholders and the Direction of the organization.**

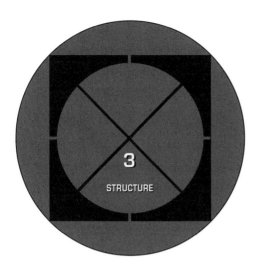

CHAPTER EIGHT
STRUCTURES AND SYSTEMS

By now, you have a good grasp of what your organization is all about. You know your reason for being — past, present and future. Your have identified and started to identify with your stakeholders, their needs and desires. You understand your strengths and weaknesses.

Now, it is time to ask: "What is the best way for us to be set up; what structures will allow us to do the things we have set out to do, and, most importantly, to meet the needs of the stakeholders of our organization?"

Warning: major paradigm shifts are possible, here.

Check your Richter scales.

Let's ask it again: what is the best way for your organization to operate? What policies, processes and procedures will make the organization most consistently responsive to your stakeholder groups?

Be ready to change.

You might find it helpful to start with some slightly different questions. Try these:

1) What is out of alignment?

2) What could be better aligned?

3) What is not supporting our stakeholders in our present environment?"

List these things.

As well, list your present processes. What are the acts of your organization, right now? What do you *do* — internally, and externally? Try to list every process that exists in your organization, from beginning to end, from warehouse to sales reps, from front door to back.

This can be time-consuming, but it is also very instructive.

List those processes, and then ask, "Given our direction as an organization, and given the needs of our stakeholders, what is out of alignment?"

The object of reviewing your processes, your organizational alignment, is to help your organization to be driven by the needs of your stakeholders, and especially the needs of your customers. In this area, the establishment of policies and processes, you must put your customers first. What are the best policies and procedures to meet their needs?

Most organizations are not structured to meet the needs of their customers. Whose needs do their processes serve? Usually, the organization!

Here is an example:

A couple plans to renovate their kitchen. They go to a local building supply centre, and tell the salesperson they want to buy hardware for their new kitchen cabinets. They're sent to the hardware department. They find the appropriate hardware, and tell salesperson number two they also need shelves. They are sent to the cabinet department, but there they discover that they really need to talk to the finished lumber salesperson. Two stops later, and loaded down with shelves and hinges, they tell the fifth salesperson they also need a faucet. They are sent to the kitchen supply department, where they can't find a salesperson, and they leave to go to another store for the rest of the items they need.

If you're smiling right now, it's probably because this scenario is distressingly familiar. Why does it happen, again and again? Because the organization is most comfortable with discrete departments, making for easier staffing, inventory control, and accounting. These meet the needs of — the organization!

But the same store, meeting the needs of the customer,

would try to find a way that the customer could deal with one sales representative (who might consult with other experts), would have their goods carried to their car, and the store would thus probably have doubled or tripled their sale to this customer couple.

Forward-thinking organizations have begun to adopt a team approach, a cross-functional, customer-driven organizational focus that cuts across traditional organizational lines to give the customer what the customer needs.

That is a paradigm shift. Your old paradigm goes right back to your days in the classroom, when you were taught to find your own answers, do your own work, to be quiet and don't talk to your neighbour. And if you looked to your neighbour for an answer, you were cheating.

It is hard to shift to a team approach where looking to your neighbour for an answer is the best way to serve your customers. But you must make that shift. You must retool the independent, individual, rigid processes and procedures, and find the flexibility and interdependence to serve your clients.

One thing that you must realize: your customers are changing, whether you are willing to change or not. Customers are demanding three things. They want it:

Faster

Better

Cheaper

In our world, today, almost all your customers have several things in common. They have fewer dollars, because the boom is over, and it isn't going to come back.

The new reality involves organizations that are watching their dollars closely, and continually re-evaluating how they are doing business. We're in a new world, a changed world.

Not only do your customers have fewer dollars, they have higher expectations. They are savvy; they know what they want, and for how much. And how soon.

And if you won't meet those three needs, they will find someone else who will! So an organization that is not focused on customer needs will not be around for very long!

Ironically, a lot of smaller organizations are already operating this "new" way, so they have no problem in this area. They are too small to have formed departments, so everyone is used to interacting. If the receptionist is on lunch or in the washroom, the boss or the stock boy will answer the phone or deal with the next customer to walk in.

But larger organizations, with complex processes and structures in place to meet the needs of the accounting department, or the managerial team, are getting hammered. They have to change, or die. They have to focus on customer needs, and set up processes to best meet *those* needs.

A key to this change is to be ready for more change — that is, to adopt processes and structures with inbuilt flexibility. One way to consider the need for flexibility, is to think of the Stakeholder groups as a stream flowing past your organization. It most likely is a fast-flowing stream. They change, their needs change, and your organization must be sufficiently flexible to move with those changes, to keep up with the flow, and continue to meet the new set of needs.

For example:

Many salespeople have been trained in specific styles of selling. Let's say Doris is highly proficient at evaluating the personality type of her client, and tailoring her approach to that type. It has worked for years.

But lately, it's not working any more. Why? Because where once her clients could be sold by pushing the proper personal interest or ego buttons, now, they are facing financial crisis. They need a salesperson who understands their new sets of needs, and who can meet them in this new arena. Doris needs to sell using creative credit policies, and value-added packages. If she will change her sales process, she may still find success. If she stays with what was once tried and true, she'll be out of the business.

Flexibility, the willingness and ability to change, is key.

Many organizations are finding their best answer, in terms of customer service, is to turn the company right on its side. Where once there were distinct departments — accounting, sales, service, transportation, manufacturing, research and development, for example — the organizational lines now run entirely the other way, bringing people from each of those former departments together as a customer-focused team. Pod people, they're called in some organizations — with pods, or teams, bringing together all the resources the customer needs. There is, of course, no one right answer, no one organizational structure that works for every situation. But you need to consider how focused you and the organization are on your customers/stakeholders, and challenge your structure in this regard.

You will also want to review your technological resources. But don't ever buy technology for fun, or because someone said it's the best there is. Invest in technology because it can help you leverage your business, it can help you meet the needs of your customers.

And be very careful that you are not saving immediate money with a technological investment that will cost you more, down the road.

One example: a company may have made an economically beneficial decision to switch from a human receptionist to a voice mail system that receives all calls, and offers seven options to the caller. That same company sees itself as customer-driven. But some customers have to wait a minute and fifteen seconds before they hear their best option (choice number seven) that sends them on to the next person — or more probably, that person's voice mail box. The process was established for financial or technological reasons, but that decision may have disregarded the needs of a key stakeholder group.

Going through the exercise of listing all processes and asking if they are in alignment, may help an organization decide to return to a human receptionist, or to streamline the voice-mail options.

We are not knocking new technology — it will help, and perhaps even save many businesses, today. But technological processes must be geared to serving the customer. Too often, with a new technological toy, we expect the customer to adapt to our new technology.

Too often, as well, we are seduced by new technology. The question should never be, "Do we have state of the art?" It should always be, "Do we have the technological resources to best serve our customers?"

It should be, "How can we do a better job for our customers with this?" Sometimes, the answer will be, we can't. Other times, your organization may find it necessary to lay out a great deal of money because the payback in customer service, and therefore customer retention, is enormous.

In the late 1970s both Emery Courier and Federal Express were faced with significant technology investment recommendations. Emery, the leading courier in the U.S. at that time, decided not to spend the money. They could not cost justify the expenditure and therefore decided not to make the investment. Federal Express on the other hand — which had less than 10% of the American market at the time — decided they had no choice. To serve their customers in the coming decades, they had to invest.

You guessed it — today, people are much more familiar with Federal Express than Emery. The investment paid off. Because it was not an investment in technology; it was an investment in customer service.

Too often, organizations undertake structural reviews,

such as we are suggesting, with the wrong end in mind. They want to eliminate jobs, or solve some internal problems. They have not considered a review in alignment with their foundation blocks. They have not reviewed with stakeholder needs in mind. The driving question in a meaningful structural review is: What is the best thing for the customer?

However, two things became apparent through working with the other areas outlined in this book:

1) An organization cannot take all of the information gained by following the plan outlined in this book, and successfully implement it, if the organization has misaligned systems. It is impossible to embrace, for example, the idea of customer service-based teams, when the people on the teams are paid totally independently, on a competitive basis that sets them one against the other. That, we concluded, is misalignment.

2) Organizations need assistance in carrying out structural reviews. That's why this chapter is included in this book, and why we work now on a regular basis in this area. We strongly suggest that organizations always evaluate systems and processes before any changes are made to structure.

A fundamental error that occurs fairly frequently is that organizations change structure first, believing that structure precedes systems. In other words, you set up the company, establish the structure, and then develop processes and systems to function within the structure that has been created.

This sounds right, but it isn't. In reality, the systems

form first, and structure tends to follow. Imagine a young organization, with two or three partners. As they work together, one naturally takes on responsibilities in his or her area of expertise; when there are gaps, someone fills it. This is all system. No one has a title, and there are no official departments yet. When the systems are working effectively, structure is identified to establish those systems in a more permanent grid. You decide who reports to whom, for example. Structure follows systems.

When you have three or five thousand employees, the same thing happens. Do not touch structure until you have evaluated the systems.

As we suggested earlier, start system evaluation by listing all the processes. Write down everything that happens in your business from one end to the other. Identify who is responsible for each thing.

By the way — there is a great side benefit to doing this work. Having this organizational systems and personnel grid is a great way to introduce a new employee into your organization. You will have an accurate map of how things work here. The newcomer will understand departmental responsibilities, and where they should go for everything they may ever need.

When you have identified all of your processes, all of your systems, ask tough questions. From the standpoint of your business:

What of this is needed; what is not.

Does this add value for our customers?

Does this make it easier or harder for our people to do their jobs?

And if you really want the answers to those questions, go out to where your people are working — on the plant floor, in the secretarial pool, in maintenance, during the sales rep meeting — and ask them one simple question:

"What is your biggest WHY?"

Like, "Why does this company make me do this?" Or, "Why do we do it this way?"

This is a great question. And when your employees talk about it, you will make some major discoveries, and you'll undoubtedly realize that there are some stupid systems within your organization. They didn't necessarily start out being stupid, but paperwork and bureaucracy have a way of taking on a life of their own, regardless of the organization around them.

A little girl once watched her Mom preparing to cook a roast. Mom carefully cut off both ends of the roast, put it in the roasting pan, and popped in into the oven. The girl asked why it was necessary to cut off the ends of the roast.

"My mother always did that," said Mom. "I assume it's because it helps the roast to cook better." The next time she saw her mother, she asked about the process, and got the identical answer — her mother had always done it.

They finally asked Grandma why she had cut the ends off the roast. "My roasting pan was too short for a big roast," said Grandma.

From that moment on, meaningless bureaucracy had taken over.

So when your employees tell you about the time-wasters, the outdated processes, the tasks done three times instead of one — LISTEN! And stop cutting the ends off the roast.

Evaluate those processes. If there is a reason for them to exist, explain this to your people. If not, turf the suckers. Don't ever again get caught up in building bureaucracy, or in manufacturing red tape — unless you're 3M.

Not all paperwork is bad. A sales system can be a useful tool to help your sales people understand what is working for them, and what isn't working. But an expense sheet that needs four signatures is make-work — you're wasting at least two people's time and energy, and telling at least three people that they have no power and are not trusted. That's a bad system.

Once you have evaluated your systems, then and only then is it time to look at your structures. You may have to change nothing at all — and this is not a make-work, with "new structures" as the desired goal. Instead, when you have redone the processes, the systems, ask if your structure supports the operation of the systems, with the focus always on the customer. Then, you may change, or you may not.

If you are planning to change structure, avoid, at all costs, talking about individual people up front in the process. Do not build a structure using individuals as pieces of a jigsaw puzzle. You will want to consult with your people concerning any structural alterations — but do not invite them to turn this into a colleague evaluation exercise: "I think Bill would do well as supervisor of a new customer service pod... Bill? He can't organize a car pool!" Don't allow this to happen. When you start getting into personalities, you get into a mess.

Build your structures on the basis of need, the need demonstrated by your systems analysis and your focus on customer service. Don't build on the basis of available human resources, especially during the consultation process involving all or some of your team members.

Develop the ideal structure. Then, using your senior managers only, evaluate the people you now have, and see where they best fit into the new structure. If they don't fit in well, don't take instant, terminal action. This is probably the time to adopt a transition plan, or to adapt the structure. Your transition plan may include working toward getting the right people so you will be able to implement the ideal structure.

To review something we mentioned in previous chapters: remember that if you are making significant changes to systems and structures — especially if you are changing reporting structures, or job responsibilities, or giving real or perceived promotions — your people will experience the consequences of change. This will disrupt people's lives; you're operating well outside their comfort zones.

So you will need to help your people manage the change process. This may mean counselling, training, coaching, re-training, and support in many ways.

If you do not provide it, you are issuing an invitation for employees to get out of alignment with your organization.

CHAPTER EIGHT: KEY NOTE REVIEW

• 'Every organization is perfectly aligned to get the results that it gets!' (Stephen Covey)

• A great plan and a worthy cause can go nowhere with systems or structures that operate in an fashion that is not aligned.

 * Actions speak louder than words.

• Structures and systems are the most difficult area to change because they are so automatically part of how we operate.

• Ask important questions about your existing systems and structures:

 * Does this system/structure add value for the Customers?

 * Does this system/structure make things easier for our people?

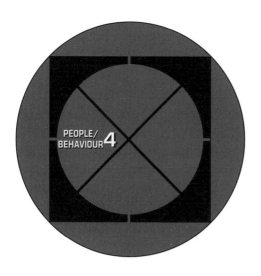

CHAPTER NINE
PEOPLE AND BEHAVIOUR

Your people are your most important asset. This easily gets forgotten in a world where you are investing in plant, or technology, or heavy-duty marketing schemes. When you're writing cheques for tens or hundreds of thousands of dollars, it's easy to forget the $350, $500 or $800 a week investment in an individual.

But remember: you can have a fantastic plant, a wonderful product, and supportive and generous owners, but if you do not have good people, the right people for your organization, you are dead in the water.

People are the key to your success.

In this chapter, we will look at two key elements in relating to those people, your team members: communication, and training. Closely related to these is the issue of personal alignment — and the downside, terminal misalignment — and we will deal with this in the next chapter.

So far, as you have applied this book to your organization, you have answered all of the big questions: Who are your stakeholders? What are their needs? What is your direction, and what should it be? What are you all about? Where are you going? You have developed a solid answer to all of these questions, and more big questions as well.

Now, we are going to look at the people you have who are going to — who must, in fact — help you to drive your organization in the direction toward those answers. You need people whose behaviour is aligned with your structure, your systems, your direction, your stakeholder needs.

How can you get your people in place, aligned with the direction of your organization, trained and effective?

Two keys: *communication*, and *personal development (training)*.

Communication

Here are some key questions for every person in your organization:

Why am I here? (What is my **PURPOSE**?)

Where am I going? (What are my **GOALS**?)

Where do I go for help? (Where do I go to find my **SUPPORT**?)

How am I doing? (Am I getting **FEEDBACK**?)

What's in it for me? (What are my **REWARDS**?)

If your people don't know the answers to those questions, they cannot become aligned with your organization.

If they know the answers on an organizational level, but do not know how they fit in, they cannot become aligned.

If they know the answers on a departmental level, but have never come to understand their role in the big picture, they cannot become aligned.

So you have to tell them and help them to become engaged.

That is the basis of the communication we're talking about here. We're not delving into psychological principles to help you relate at the deepest level to your team members — we're talking about developing a system of communication that will ensure that every member of your team knows where they fit into the big picture.

It's an ongoing process, because you need to check back on a regular basis.

And it is essential, because if the department doesn't know where it fits into the larger organization, and the individual doesn't know where he or she fits into the department, then you have a guaranteed recipe for ineffi-ciency, at best, and complete corporate meltdown, at worst.

Each one of your people needs to know what their role is, how that role fits into the role of their department, and how their role and that of the department fits into the organization as a whole.

And you have to tell them and provide the opportunity of seeing how their job fits into the big picture.

You need to build lots of opportunities to tell them — beginning with understanding their role in the organiza-tion, and connected to daily interaction, weekly meetings, monthly reviews, team meetings, quarterly reviews, and annual performance appraisals. Each and all of these pre-sent opportunities to bring your people into alignment.

As well, your communication practices and systems need to have internal alignment. You need to understand that every communication opportunity — from one-minute conversations to performance appraisals — must be a step toward organizational alignment.

What is your job?

A basic question that can open the kind of communica-tion we're talking about is: "What is your job?"

That is vital first step in developing a performance agreement with your people — and the performance agreement is an understanding or document that serves as a map toward organizational alignment. The perfor-mance agreement — which will outline the job, and the measures by which success or lack of success in it will be determined — must be consistent with the overall performance direction of the department and the organization.

So you can start by asking your employee: "What is your job?" When they have formulated their answer, discuss with them their vision of their job as it fits into the bigger picture. Your goal, here, is to be in agreement about this; failure to agree means you are starting out of alignment.

Let's be clear that agreement does not imply a democratic vote on the job description. Discussion between manager and employee does not imply equal voices. Eventually, if you don't agree on all things, communication ceases to be two-way and becomes directive. If you're a manager, part of your job is to set out these kinds of guidelines, and to deal with today's realities, so your people are driving your organization in an aligned fashion.

Far and away, the easiest time to be directive, and to establish a clear performance agreement, is at the time of hiring. However, the same approach must be taken with any employee, regardless of seniority.

But let's consider an example concerning a new employee at a newspaper. She's been hired to be a reporter. She understands that her job description is, "write news stories for the newspaper." But this has not yet been quantified; no performance agreement is in place.

One element of the agreement will concern quantity of stories. So you start the two-way discussion. You ask what she sees her job as being. *"Writing news stories."* That's good — you agree, so far.

"How many news stories?" you ask.

"I think three stories a week would be good," she says.

At this point, as the publisher of a weekly newspaper, you move toward directive communication.

"I understand that you would like to write three stories a week. But let me give you the big picture. For our newspaper to exist, we need to publish 40 pages a week. Those pages will include, on average, 60% advertising, and 40% news. We rely on three reporters to supply 75% of the materials to fill that 'news hole'. My math tells me that you need to provide stories to fill four pages a week, on average. That will amount to between 12 and 20 stories a week."

"But I would feel comfortable writing three."

"Maybe you would. But we need between 12 and 20. That is not negotiable. Maybe writing three would meet the needs of another newspaper — I'm not saying it's right or wrong. But here, we need between 12 and 20."

This may be a conversation or a discussion, but it is also directed by you. You know where you must go with it, to achieve alignment. The number of stories is set, not by your whim, but by the needs of your newspaper. It is based on the foundation, on the needs and the value system of your organization. It sets out, clearly and explicitly, how you operate in that organization.

If you have a family, this scenario will be familiar:

"Clean your room."

"Why?"

"Because this family is founded on some principles, and one of them is neatness. Our direction is to have a neat house, and your role is to keep your part of this house clean."

"Okay, I'll clean it once a week."

"No, every day."

"I don't want to."

"I understand your feelings. We have 'realities' that we need to deal with that sometimes are not easy to accept. We also have roles and responsibilities to accept. Not everything we do or need to do is a pleasant task. However, keeping your room clean once a week is not an acceptable time frame, in terms of fulfilling our family principles. Therefore, daily is what is required."

Let's return, for a moment, to our earlier discussion of empowerment. Here is a good analogy. If — to the parent's shock — the room is clean, every day, for a couple of weeks, the parent will probably stop checking as often. The assigned task will now include trust — the basic definition of empowerment. The child will feel good that he is being trusted to do what he's been told to do, without daily check-ups. Trust grows, confidence grows, relationship grows.

That's in an ideal world. However, an empowered child who takes the opportunity to slack off is being irresponsible, and is acting out of alignment with the household. Remember, irresponsibility is the mortal enemy of empowerment.

Empowerment must be linked with personal responsibility and alignment. A paycheque is not all we should earn, on the job. We should also be earning trust.

And communication is key to establishing the expectation of personal responsibility, and the direction of alignment. Through communication, the manager and the employee work together toward alignment and responsibility and thus, toward empowerment.

If the employee has demonstrated personal responsibility and is in alignment, but is not being trusted with present tasks or offered further responsibility, the manager is failing.

If the employee is empowered, but is not performing adequately or responsibly under the decreased supervision, both the employee and the manager are failing.

Some managers are afraid to trust their people, because a failure falls on both employee and manager. That may be understandable, but it is also shortsighted. Managers need to trust and empower their employees — gradually, with checks and balances. Employees need to accept these opportunities responsibly, and have a strong desire to perform the tasks within their job in order to be sure they are working in alignment with the big organizational picture.

This can take time to develop, especially in an organization with a history of no empowerment, managers who make all decisions, and employees who have been invited to check their brains at the door.

The starting point, as in any organizational situation, is communication. "Here is what we are all about." "Here is where we want to go." "Here is where you fit into that picture."

You must help your people to understand where they fit in, in this organization. You must systematically shape your communication opportunities — from coffee conversation to annual performance review — to this end.

There are two frequent errors that must be avoided:

1) *Settling for "natural", informal communication, only.* "Do I talk to my people? Sure! We talk every day; they're always in and out of my office." This is fine, as far as it goes, but it can leave tremendous gaps, with only half the staff knowing a key piece of information. It also tends to focus on the immediate and the urgent, and ignore the big picture.

2) *Engaging only in crisis communication.* This casts your communication as negative and crisis-driven. It also tends to be focused on details, missing the big picture.

You can practice — with positive results, by the way — on yourself. The next time you are faced with a crisis, force yourself to pause, and think about the big picture. It will probably change how you feel about the current situation, and your role in it.

For example: "I can't believe it! The damned phone's ringing again. *What? Your shipment didn't arrive? That's not my fault — I sent it to you Tuesday! All right, I'll find out.* Who does he think I am, anyway?"

Your afternoon, your mood, and the size of your future orders from that customer are all headed straight down.

But what if you had done this: "I can't believe it! The damned phone's ringing again... (Pause: What's the big picture, here? Our company exists because of our customers. Without them, there is no company. My role is to serve those customers...) Hello? You have a problem? I'm sorry — how can I help you?"

Placing yourself in the big picture, even during a crisis, can really lend some important perspective, and help you act in alignment with the direction of your organization. In fact, you may realize that part of your proper role is as a crisis solver — that certainly would change your reaction and your approach.

The same principle is true with your people, and in situations where the crisis involves your people.

Stop focusing on the crisis, or the individual incidents, and place them in their context in the big picture.

In our informal world, it may seem foreign to think about communication in such a formal, thought-through sense. Especially when one of the messages of this book is to become more flexible.

But careful, comprehensive communication is key to alignment. And without alignment, your organization is operating, at best, under an extreme handicap.

So although you will undoubtedly communicate spontaneously, be sure you also communicate regularly, on schedule, through individual meetings, team meetings, performance reviews and other built-in communication opportunities. And keep the big picture in mind, even in informal communication.

Review with your people how they as individuals fit in, and how you will measure their success. Do the same with your department and your organization. For illustration purposes, consider this diagram:

*The flow goes both ways.

The frequency is determined by each situation. Some new employees will need a check-in every day, then, every week. Some empowered people may need a scheduled contact every month or even every quarter.

Do not stretch it out too far. It's like flying a plane across the country — you want to check frequently to be sure you're on course.

The fundamental problem with many performance appraisal systems is that this sort of communication happens only once a year. There has been no checking in, no course correction. They left New York for Paris, and the first hint of something being wrong was when they landed in Los Angeles. Wondering about that big river in the middle of the country might have helped. Questioning the lack of ocean immediately after take-off would have solved the alignment problem even earlier.

It is all part of communication. Have performance appraisals, sure, but make them part of your larger communication system that includes informal conversations, team meetings, monthly conversations, and all of the other "big picture" opportunities that will help to bring your people into alignment.

Personal Development (Training)

You need your people. You need them to perform at a certain level of competence to get the job done. How do you achieve this acceptable level of behaviour? That's where the development process is important. This may include training.

Before we consider the area of training, keep in mind that the "development process" is an ongoing journey that includes the day-to-day lessons we learn from our experiences. In considering the "change process", as an example, let us examine the broader perspective of development, and where the training component fits in.

For a person to change, there needs to be something of deep value to the individual in order for him or her to incorporate the change. The change itself will come about from utilizing the experiences that we have had that reflect upon the change, as well as any new learnings that we made need, i.e. training. In this example, we see that training represents one element of the change process including utilizing the life experiences or lessons that we have learned.

You need to ask, what training do you need for your people, for your departments, for your organization at large to fit properly within your structures and systems, to work in your direction, to meet your needs? In other words, to be in alignment.

Let's underline this: the training you offer needs to be aligned with the rest of the organization, and with the understanding your people have of your direction. Too often, organizations plan what you might call "training in a vacuum" — they offer a course or a seminar that may be a good idea, but they do not align it with the organizational big picture.

So the employees show up for another training course that has little or no apparent connection with their job. They need to have that understanding — they need to understand, through effective communication, where they fit in, in this organization, and then they need to know how this training is going to help them in that role.

An example: in a recent planning session held with a management team, one of the managers made a very contextual statement. Having completed the analysis of the Stakeholders, having established the foundation blocks, future picture and issues, and having discussed the structures of the organization, she now had a much better appreciation of her specific development needs. She mentioned that she had attended many training sessions in the past, but now she knew what her needs were, based on a much deeper understanding of what the organization was all about, where it is going and why it is set up the way it is. Her role and responsibilities are much clearer.

Out of context training is a huge waste of time, energy and money on the part of the company, because a person needs to have a clear understanding of why he or she needs to be trained, before any effective training can occur. So be sure that everyone going into a training opportunity understands where that training fits into the big picture, and how it will help them fit better into the big picture.

It is imperative, for any training to be effective, that it is aligned with the organizational structures, direction, and the needs of the stakeholders. When considering training requirements within the organization, reflect on the needs that were identified in the analysis of the other elements leading up to this area. Perhaps you will require training due to new skill requirements that are a result of structural changes. Or perhaps there will be need for development in the customer service area. There are many possibilities, but they need to be in alignment with the stakeholder needs, direction, and organizational structure and systems.

It is unfortunate that, in today's challenging economy, some organizations are cutting back on training. We may be biased, but we believe that training is becoming more, not less, essential.

You have a number of different resources that are required to run your business. The more resources you have, the higher the cost of obtaining and operating those resources, and the more important it is that you have high quality people operating those resources.

It makes no sense to spend money on capital expenditures if you are not going to have your best people trained in the best way to make the best use of those resources.

In North America today, the current paradigm is "cut training". It's a mistake, a bad paradigm. With the rate and magnitude of change that you and your people are facing, training, upgrading and retooling are important keys to your success.

But please understand that training does not have to be a dollar-intensive exercise. There needs to be more creativity in the training area. You can continue a training program but cut back your financial commitment to it by adopting train-one-another programs, and accessing value-added programs where clients or suppliers will provide training. Don't automatically pay for the training on the new program, get it as part of the package from the supplier, if you can.

The true test of effective training is not the dollars you spend on it. It is the result — is this training bringing your people into alignment with your organizational direction; is it equipping them to be a more effective resource in your company's big picture?

If you are a manager reading this book, and you're planning to put this process into action in your organization, may we suggest that a cost-effective training approach would be to provide a copy of the book to each of your people. Then they will understand where you are going, and they will have a resource that will greatly facilitate organizational alignment. You'll be reading from the same blueprint.

To return to a familiar theme: everything we have talked about so far involves some kind of change. Human beings need help in adapting to change. Train your managers and your employees about change — how to adapt to a changing environment, how to help your people adapt; the consequences of change.

Remember — if you are changing your structures, you often can do that pretty quickly. But while the organizational changes may be in place three months from now, the impact on your people may not manifest itself for six months or a year.

You can greatly lessen that impact by training, preparing your team for change and guiding them through it.

CHAPTER NINE: KEY NOTE REVIEW

• Every manager should know that their team knows the answers to the following questions:

* Why are we here?	- PURPOSE
* Where are we going?	- GOALS
* Where do I go for help?	- SUPPORT
* How am I doing?	- FEEDBACK
* What is in it for me?	- REWARDS

• When communicating about structure/direction/stakeholder needs, state it in the terms of what this means to the individual's roles and responsibilities, and how they are affecting the organization's success.

• Empowerment means ownership of a particular job or task. In order to have ownership there needs to be trust established, which is directly connected to the competence of the individuals involved and how they have behaved in the past.

• For training to be effective, the individual needs to know why the skill development area is important and how it fits into the big picture for the organization or their department.

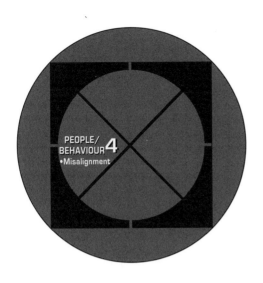

CHAPTER TEN
DEALING WITH MISALIGNMENT

In this chapter, we remain with the topic of people and behaviour. We have set this theme of dealing with misalignment in a separate chapter not because it is unrelated to the previous chapter, but because it is so important, and thus demands individual attention.

Stated more bluntly: this is probably the toughest area for any organization to deal with, so you need to focus carefully on it.

Keep in mind that 'every organization is perfectly aligned to get the results that it gets!'

Look ahead with us to six months or a year from now. You have worked through the process of moving your entire organization toward alignment. You have walked through the steps, putting each into practice.

Once upon a time, you used to dread hiring new people. Now, with a clear view of your organization, your needs, your vision, your values and your goals, hiring new staff has become much easier — you know what you are looking for in a new employee. You know what their role will be, and how they will fit into the structure.

You hire with all of these things in mind. You hire people who are going to be aligned with your organization.

We are not going to explore the details, here, other than to say: Hire with your value base in mind. Hire people who can work within your new, revised or existing structures. Hire people who are excited about your business.

Don't just hire people who need a job — hire people who are enthused about working in the business that you are enthused about!

There are lots of useful helps around concerning the hiring process. Just be sure you hire from the foundation we have discussed all through this book, and hiring will be much less of a challenge than it once was.

Now, instead, your biggest personnel problem involves existing employees who so far have resisted moving in your overall organizational direction. How do you deal with them? And now you discover you have some people who haven't walked that road with you. Your organization has changed, but they have not.

Let's start by examining your goal, in these cases. Is it to get them out the door? Or is it to get them aligned with the organization, if that's possible? We suspect that in most cases, your first choice will be door number two.

This will, in many instances, involve highly effective communication, training at the highest level, and patience. That's because as a leader, you are helping your people to do a serious self-evaluation, and in this way work through their own personal alignment. You are helping them to discover if your organization is where they want to be, where they want to contribute, where their commitment and their energies will be placed. In other words: are they ready, willing and able to become aligned?

Let's keep one thing clearly in mind: there are only two roads here — alignment, or exit. Too often, the reality is that people try to follow a third path: they quit, and stay. They shut down, but keep picking up the paycheque. They do the minimum necessary to keep their job — and in some organizations, especially big ones, the minimum daily requirement is awfully minimal.

We need to help these on-the-job retirees, and anyone else resisting alignment, to ask themselves some honest questions:

"Is this job the right place for me?"

"Is my heart in this, and if not, could it be?"

If the answer to these is "no", a number of options still exist for you and your employee. The final solution is, of course, for you to part company.

But before we come to that, let's look at some alternatives.

Is the employee out of alignment because they are not the right person for the job, or because they do not have the right tools to do the job?

If the latter is true, you have a training issue, first of all. You may be able to give the employee the right tools through training, and you may be amazed at how a mis-aligned employee becomes entirely aligned to your organizational directions, once he or she is able to successfully fulfill an assigned role that fits their skill base, and to enjoy the rewards of succeeding.

Or, is the employee out of alignment because they are wrong for that job, but could be right in another position in the company? Too often, especially in our ever-changing organizational environments, people are shunted into jobs they did not ask for, far removed from the roles they first filled in the company. Give some attention to aligning a person with the right job, before you decide that person should be shown the door.

And always remember the famous "Peter Principle" which suggests that people are promoted to their level of incompetence — a sure way to have mis-aligned people. Before you conclude someone is wrong for your company, be sure they are not simply wrong for their particular position.

If these internal shifts are not the solution, help your employee to turn the question around. Do not ask, "Am I wrong for the job." Ask, instead, "Is this job wrong for me?"

This is not just a word game. Often, an employee and a job may seem to be a good match, but something continues to be out of alignment. Here's an example:

A university graduate takes a job on the fast stream in a corporation. He has all the skills, the smarts and the intuition to make it all the way to the board room. He's headed for the top, as long as he is prepared to put in the extra hours, take work home with him, and make several business trips each quarter.

But he has been married for a year and a half, and the couple has a month-old baby. He has aimed for this job ever since he entered business school but, just now, his new family is more important to him.

In one sense, he is right for the job. But in reality, this job, right now, is wrong for him.

A visionary company would look for opportunities that align with the individual's needs. Or, the company may help him to decide that he cannot come into alignment with the job and the organization, and so he must look elsewhere for employment.

Your company would be wise to invest in training for people who are apparently out of alignment. Give them a chance to evaluate their place in the organization, their personal mission, their direction, their values.

Everyone will be happier if the employees either come into alignment with your organization, or decide, with the help of resources you provide, that they need to look elsewhere.

But this is not to suggest that the decision is ultimately up to them. In many cases, your organizational leaders will ultimately have to make the tough calls. And it is fundamentally important that you do.

Think of your organization as a sports team. We've all known of teams where 20 players are absolutely committed to following the coach's system, playing the way he says, meeting the needs of the team and the fans. But if there are four or five players who don't buy into that system, who dog it or play for their own glory, the team will never know success.

In fact, you don't really even have a team! You have misalignment, and you're heading for one of three results.

The team fails to achieve its goals; or

The misaligned players are cut or traded; or

The coach gets fired.

Think about it.

Cutting a team member is a tough job. For most managers, it's the hardest item on their job description. But you have to have the toughness to finally put the organization ahead of the individual. If nothing else works — training, communication, advice, job transfer — you must be determined to have alignment, and you must make that happen.

Ultimately, the leader must make that decision, and take that action.

But let us caution you: because most of us find this very difficult, we tend to cut and run — hand over the pink slip, and hide in our office for the rest of the day. That's not the way to go. If someone must be dropped from your team, make their landing as soft as possible. Be empathetic. Give them training opportunities or direction, to help them find a new job. Unless they are being fired for cause — which is not the scenario we're discussing, here — help them find leads to new jobs, and give honest but positive references.

Their departure does not mean they are necessarily bad; it means they did not fit into your organization. Not everyone will.

Departmental alignment

Misalignment is a problem that can occur with departments, as well as individuals.

Perhaps the most common example occurs when departments ignore the fact that their stakeholders include other departments. When they think about being customer-focused — if they do — they think in external terms, only.

But let us caution you: because most of us find this very difficult, we tend to cut and run — hand over the pink slip, and hide in our office for the rest of the day. That's not the way to go. If someone must be dropped from your departments thought and acted in those terms. This is possible, but only if departments go through the same kind of programs — through communication and through training — that individuals do.

If you are an accountant, please stick with us through the next few paragraphs — they may be painful, but they also should help.

We include this somewhat tongue-in-cheek warning because accounting departments are often the first to forget that the other parts of the organization are their customers. Because the accountants are often the inventors of the organization's systems, those systems are often set up to work well for the accounting department. Too often, though, the "Biggest Why" question we referred to in the previous chapter involves awkward or redundant demands placed on other departments by the accounting department.

In far too many organizations the accounting department has a mentality in common with a police state. Too often, an organization commits much time, energy, and even financial resources to an employee empowerment effort which fails utterly when it hits the steel doors of the accounting department.

Remember, empowerment is a job or task with trust; accounting departments, and many middle and senior managers, are expert at asking the questions that illustrate a high degree of mistrust.

Accounting departments — and all other departments in your organization — need to change their paradigm. The other departments are not the enemy, or the competitor, or the thorn in the flesh. They are your internal customer, and your attitudes and your systems should reflect that new reality.

This new reality is to work at ensuring that all systems

within the organization are connected to one another and support a meaningful purpose in their being.

Maintaining alignment

Remember the last time you painted your house, or vacuumed your car? Take a look at it now — how did it deteriorate to its present condition?

This happens all around us — we get something in perfect working order, and then we take that perfection for granted. Before long, things aren't in such good shape.

That is exactly the situation with a properly aligned organization. You bring it into alignment. You make sure your people are aligned. You make sure your departments are aligned.

But then, you need a mechanism to hold the ground you have gained, to maintain your organizational alignment.

Alignment is not a one-time, once-for-all matter. You can't fix it once and ignore it ever after. Checking for misalignment must be an ongoing process in your organization, especially because of the changes, and the rate of those changes, that your organization faces on an ongoing basis.

You must always be checking to see that people and departments are in alignment. You must be sure they haven't slipped back into old patterns, and that as new challenges and opportunities come to your organization, you respond to them consistently, in alignment with your organizational direction.

In other words, you must continually be seeking renewal, individually, departmentally, and organizationally.

That is the focus of our next chapter.

CHAPTER TEN: KEY NOTE REVIEW

• The ongoing and continual process of aligning all elements within your organization will drive the overall levels of success of the organization. This is not only a short term focus, but should represent reality in both the short and long term.

• Alignment deals with individuals, departments and organizations 'self-correcting' in the following areas:

   * Direction
   * Understanding of the Stakeholder needs
   * Structures and systems and processes
   * Behaviour
   * Personal Development (Training)

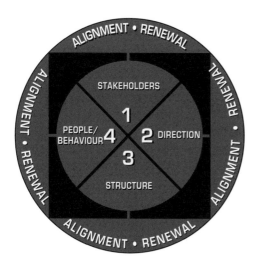

CHAPTER ELEVEN
RENEWAL

Think of renewal as maintaining and improving on success. As we stated at the end of the preceding chapter, you cannot take for granted the success you have now found. You must work to maintain it, and improve on it.

This is true individually, departmentally, and organizationally. And you need to have a system in place to ensure that renewal is not forgotten.

Individual renewal

How do you ensure your alignment, and that of the people for whom you are responsible, on a day to day basis? Because, if you achieve this, then you are going to be in very fine shape, organizationally.

We suggest that you schedule time, every day or, at least, every week, to look at your organization's "big picture", and to evaluate how you and your department are doing, relative to that picture.

Every week, at least, you should plan for time to remind yourself of the needs of the stakeholders, and of the direction of your organization; and you will quickly but effectively evaluate how you, and your department, are doing in terms of being in alignment with that picture. You will ask questions like:

Am I going in the same direction as this organization?

What is my mission?

Am I missing anything?

Am I remembering the needs of my stakeholders — external and internal?

As well, get into the habit of taking a pause in crisis situations to ask yourself two questions:

Where does this issue fit into the big picture?

Is our response or solution in alignment with our organization's direction?

To give a practical example of this:

Imagine an irate phone call from a customer, who has — it does happen, doesn't it? — a terrible attitude. What is your first reaction to this situation? Anger, frustration, a desire to make it an early day? That might be ours, too.

But pause, and ask yourself: *Where does this fit into the big picture?* Well, the customer is a key stakeholder.

What response would be in alignment with your organization's direction? The best effort you can make at serving this customer.

This is not magic — the client may still wind up angry or with a bad attitude. But he will certainly have dealt with a very different attitude at your end because you paused to glance at the big picture. Unless he is entirely unreasonable, he will know your organization values him as a customer, and is eager to listen to and respond to his issues.

You will have made him feel as good as possible, in the situation, about your organization. That's a good habit to get into, isn't it?

Organizational renewal

You must also check, often and thoroughly, to be sure your organization stays on track. It's very much like the aftermath of a diet or an exercise program — how often do we fail to check ourselves, on a regular basis, only to be surprised 12 months later that we have regained the weight and lost the muscle tone?

Do not let this happen, organizationally. You need to revisit the process you have just followed, on a regular basis. We suggest it should happen formally on an annual basis. Once a year, walk through all the steps that you

183

have taken through this book.

Obviously, it won't take as much time or energy as the first time, because you have already done the hard work of getting on track, this time around. But don't take it lightly, either, because falling out of alignment, losing sight of your stakeholders or your direction, will immediately cost you efficiency and effectiveness.

You will probably find that reviewing areas one and two — *stakeholders*, and *direction* — will basically be a memory check. Little will change, in these areas, and your review will be a reminder of who the stakeholders are, and what the direction is that you have set for your organization. Change is possible, but wide-reaching change is unlikely.

In areas three and four — *systems and structure*, and *people and behaviour* — you should be continually reviewing and refining. In one sense, these areas represent the tools by which you bring to pass what you have defined in areas one and two, and you will want to use the opportunity to maintain, hone, and improve those tools on a regular basis.

You will want to ask some questions about the review process.

How often will you undergo this organizational check-up?

We mentioned a year, but we also believe that if the pace of change is rapid in your organization, you may want to have an organization-wide check-up more often than that. It won't take long but, unlike the individual renewal, it

184

ensures that the entire organization gets an alignment once-over that could save you from a lot of grief.

How will you tie renewal into other areas of planning?

You may find it ideal to begin your planning cycle with a check-up, before you look ahead in formulating detailed operational plans.

Who should be involved?

Perhaps, as you have brought your organization through this process this first time, your senior managers have been primarily involved, and you have simply communicated the changes to your people. Renewal may be the opportunity to broaden this base of involvement.

There are no well-defined, all-inclusive answers to these questions. Your method of organizational renewal will have to be tailored to your organization.

There is, however, one wrong answer: *do nothing.*

The challenges of the journey

We believe that, as you have walked with us, following this map to organizational effectiveness, you have already grasped the exciting, positive potential for your own organization or business.

So we conclude with seven key thoughts: as you bring this plan into reality in your organization, here are seven areas that present the greatest challenges to your success. By being aware of these, you will sidestep some of the major roadblocks to success.

The toughest obstacles to organizational effectiveness:

1) Putting the time necessary into evaluating stakeholder needs. It all starts here, and if you have not spent the time and effort to have a valid list of stakeholders, and a complete understanding of their needs, you are starting the process at a crippling disadvantage.

2) Real engagement of direction: foundation, vision, and goals. This is not an academic exercise. You and your team need to take this as seriously as if you were starting a new company, with everything you own and can borrow invested in it. If that were the case, what would be the foundation, the vision and the goals of this organization? Take this exactly that seriously, and give it just as much attention and focus.

3) Genuine evaluation of structures and systems. It is easy to continue with the status quo. It is hard, and even threatening, to change how things operate. But you must approach this evaluation with a willingness to change any and all things, if it is necessary for your success.

4) Dealing with misalignment. No one likes confrontation with employees. And while your motive is to help the employee and the organization, carrying this out is not easy, nor pleasant. But it must be done, or you will have the ideal company on paper, on your shelf, but the old clunker dying a slow death on the factory floor and in the offices.

5) Connecting training to organizational effectiveness. Too many training efforts are disconnected, offered because they are easy and available, not because they meet needs identified through this organization-deep process.

6) Communicating in a consistent and structured fashion concerning what you are building. Your communication patterns may be haphazard and entirely informal — here, too, you need a paradigm shift to cause a shift in practice. If your people don't know what your organization is all about, they are entirely unable to perform in alignment with your organizational direction.

7) Managing and coping with change. You know that the changes you will make will help avoid even greater changes associated with failure, somewhere down the road. That doesn't make change any easier to deal with, and everyone in your organization may need some assistance in accepting change and in performing effectively in the midst of the new business realities.

Nobody likes change. But everyone enjoys success.

As you put this guidebook to organizational effectiveness into practice in your organization, you will discover both of those statements to be basic, fundamental truths.

And as you follow the steps toward gaining and maintaining organizational alignment, you will discover that you have indeed helped to guide your organization toward optimum growth and success.

All the best as your journey unfolds.

THE FIX:

How to align your organization for growth and success

Special discount rates are available for organizations and businesses buying in quantity for their staff and/or clients.

To place your order, or to learn more about the services provided by FUSION Consulting Inc., contact:

**FUSION Consulting Inc.,
3 Lansdowne Park Cr.,
P.O. Box 236,
Komoka, Ontario
N0L 1R0**

**Telephone (519) 657-1870
1-800-465-5871 (in Canada)
Fax (519) 641-2038**